What the Bible Says About...

Katie M Cal

2 Timothy 3:16-17

Katie Erickson

ISBN: 9781792735363

Dedication

This book is dedicated to you, the reader, to encourage you to continue being curious as you explore the one true authority on all topics: the Bible.

I especially want to thank my parents, Bill and Mary Schott, for raising me with a great Biblical foundation and a love for God and His Word. Your encouragement and support for all of the ministry work I'm involved with means the world to me!

I also want to thank Jason DeZurik of the Worldview Warriors ministry for encouraging me to write these first as blog posts and then to put them in book format. I appreciate that this ministry has provided me with a platform to share my passion for God's Word.

- Katie Erickson

Table of Contents

Why the Bible?

This book contains writings published on the Worldview Warriors blog on various topics and what the Bible says about them, to help us all stay grounded in a Biblical foundation in life.

But before we just jump into topics, we need to dig into why the Bible can be trusted as an authority on all of these topics. Why the Bible? Why not any other book, person, etc.?

Everyone has different people or things in their life that they consider to be an authority. Each source of authority can have little or a lot of weight in life, depending how much we count on them to advise and inform our worldview.

My standard mode of operations to share on the authority of the Bible is to look within the Bible itself. Some may say this is circular logic, but what better source is there than the inspired word of God Himself? The assumptions in this are that God exists and that the Bible IS His inspired Word. I believe those two points, partly because I have no reason not to. God has proven that He exists and is God, and as His creation, I trust the Word of the supreme Creator of the universe. These are the assumptions I'm coming from in writing this, so please take that into consideration as you read on.

On that note, what does the Bible say about its own authority?

2 Timothy 3:16-17 says, "All Scripture is God-breathed and is useful for teaching, rebuking, correcting and training in righteousness, so that the servant of God may be thoroughly equipped for every good work."

2 Peter 1:20-21 says, "Above all, you must understand that no prophecy of Scripture came about by the prophet's own interpretation of things. For prophecy never had its origin in the human will, but prophets, though human, spoke from God as they were carried along by the Holy Spirit."

These passages show that the Bible was given to us by God Himself, both through His direct speech to humankind and through divine inspiration. There are over 4,000 times in the Bible that God speaks directly to humankind! All of the writers of Scripture were divinely inspired by God Himself regarding what to write. They may not have had direct knowledge of certain historical events they were writing about, but God inspired them with all of the information they needed. Because of God's divine inspiration, the Bible is inerrant in its original autographs.

So what if someone wants to test these claims about the Bible? Well, approximately 2500 years ago, God spoke such a test through the prophet Isaiah. Check out the following passages:

"'Present your case,' says the Lord. 'Set forth your arguments,' says Jacob's King. 'Tell us, you idols, what is going to happen. Tell us what the former things were, so that we may consider them and know their final outcome. Or declare to us the things to come, tell us what the future holds, so we may know that you are gods. Do something, whether good or bad, so that we will be dismayed and filled with fear. But you are less than nothing and your works are utterly worthless; whoever chooses you is detestable.'" (**Isaiah 41:21-24**)

"I am the Lord; that is my name! I will not yield my glory to another or my praise to idols. See, the former things have taken place, and new things I declare; before they spring into being I announce them to you." (**Isaiah 42:8-9**)

"This is what the Lord says—Israel's King and Redeemer, the Lord Almighty: I am the first and I am the last; apart from me there is no God. Who then is like me? Let him proclaim it. Let him declare and lay out before me what has happened since I established my ancient people, and what is yet to come—yes, let them foretell what will come. Do not tremble, do not be afraid. Did I not proclaim this and foretell it long ago? You are my witnesses. Is there any God besides me? No, there is no other Rock; I know not one." (**Isaiah 44:6-8**)

"Remember the former things, those of long ago; I am God, and there is no other; I am God, and there is none like me. I make known the end from the beginning, from ancient times, what is still to come. I say, 'My purpose will stand, and I will do all that I please.' From the east I summon a bird of prey; from a far-off land, a man to fulfill my purpose. What I have said, that I will bring about; what I have planned, that I will do." (**Isaiah 46:9-11**)

These passages show us that we can test the Bible by testing its claims, and looking at history to see whether the events it foretold have come to pass (spoiler alert: they have!). The only way that ALL of the many prophecies in the Bible could have come to fruition in the manner that they did is if the prophecies were divinely inspired.

There is so much more that has been written and that we could write on regarding this topic of "Why the Bible?". If you're seeking and wondering why you should believe the Bible as true and authoritative in your life, I encourage you to contact Worldview Warriors at our website (WorldviewWarriors.org) or on our Facebook page. We'd love to talk with you more about this!

What the Bible Says About
Heaven

What does the Bible say about heaven? A lot, actually. First of all, heaven was created by God: "In the beginning, God created the heavens and the earth" (**Genesis 1:1**). God created the earth as a dwelling place for His people (more on that in a future section), and the heavens as the place where God was to dwell. After the fall of mankind in **Genesis 3**, heaven became a place that humans could no longer go without a right relationship with God. God cannot be in the presence of sin, and humans had sinned. Heaven (and more importantly the presence of God there) is where we should all long to be, because it is a perfect place, free of any sort of sin or evil (**Revelation 21-22**).

While heaven may be known as a big, big house with lots and lots of rooms, that is essentially how Jesus Himself described it. **John 14:1-3** says, "'Do not let your hearts be troubled. You believe in God; believe also in me. My Father's house has many rooms; if that were not so, would I have told you that I am going there to prepare a place for you? And if I go and prepare a place for you, I will come back and take you to be with me that you also may be where I am."

How do we get to heaven? Jesus answers that question, just a few verses after the previous passage, in **John 14:6**: "Jesus answered, 'I am the way and the truth and the life. No one comes to the Father except through me.'" We know that Jesus Christ will reign in heaven, seated at the right hand of God, and we will get to go there to join Him if we have faith in Him (**Colossians 3:1-4**).

We learn a number of things about heaven (and hell - more on that in the next section) from the parable of the rich man and Lazarus in **Luke 16:19-31**. We know that a person cannot cross between the two. Heaven is the reward for those who have faith, and our life circumstances on earth don't matter there. This is the only passage where we see any correspondence between the two sides of heaven and hell.

Read **Revelation 21-22** for a pretty detailed description of what heaven will look like and its physical characteristics. But remember that language is limiting; John (the author of Revelation) probably had no words to describe the majesty, glory, and perfection of the glimpse of heaven that he got to experience. Our limited human minds and vocabulary just can't grasp or understand the complete and inexplicable brilliance of this glorious place!

Have you ever wondered about **Revelation 21:1**, which says, "Then I saw a new heaven and a new earth, for the first heaven and the first earth had passed away, and there was no longer any sea." This same idea is echoed earlier in **Isaiah 65:17-25**. The new earth makes sense, since this one is full of sin. But why a new heaven? The answer is in the concept of the current heaven versus the eternal heaven.

The current heaven is the heaven that exists right now, where all believers in Jesus who have physically died now exist. We who believe will all go to the current heaven when we physically die, assuming Jesus' second coming has not yet happened. The current heaven is like when you're waiting to get into a really great concert, but they haven't opened the doors yet; it's still awesome to be there, but it's not quite the main event yet.

We know that if we have faith, we will get to go to the current heaven immediately when we die (**Luke 23:39-43**). What's happening in the current heaven? We can eat from the tree of life (**Revelation 2:7**) and experience that eternal life that is promised to us. Those who have been killed for their faith are there, crying out for justice on earth and praying (**Revelation 6:9-11**). The saints there will serve God day and night, they will never hunger or thirst, and they will not have any sorrow (**Revelation 7:13-17**).

So what's the deal with the new heaven then? The new heaven is the eternal heaven that will happen after the second coming of Jesus. This is like when the concert doors finally open and you're let into the main event – but it will be way beyond the most amazing thing you can imagine! This is the house of many rooms that Jesus spoke of in **John 14:1-3**. We know from **Matthew 22:23-33** that earthly family relationships really won't matter there since we're all the family of God. We as believers will get to live on forever there (**Isaiah 66:22**). The eternal heaven is where God's righteousness dwells (**2 Peter 3:13**). If we have followed Jesus in this life, we will receive our eternal reward there (**Matthew 19:28-30**).

Do we know exactly what heaven will look like? Nope. But do the details really matter? If you're only concerned about things like how big your room there will be or who will get the room next to yours, then I'd encourage you to check your focus. The point of heaven is for God's creation to finally be able to dwell with Him forever and spend our days doing the best thing ever - giving glory to God. How awesome is that!

What the Bible Says About
Hell

In the previous section, we discussed what the Bible says about heaven, and we briefly touched on the idea of hell. Here, we're looking a bit more into hell and what the Bible says about it.

One of the primary texts we have regarding hell is the parable of the rich man and Lazarus in **Luke 16:19-31**. Lazarus goes to heaven and is by Abraham's side, but the rich man goes to hell and is in constant suffering there. What is hell like for him? Well, a drop of water to cool his tongue sounds to him like the most amazing thing he could ever have. I've gotten pretty thirsty at times, but that sounds pretty severe! He is also tormented by the fact that his family members will likely suffer the same fate as him, but there's nothing he can do about it. Finally, the icing on the cake so to speak is that we know he can see heaven. That would be like being so close to that refreshing water in a time of extreme thirst, and even seeing someone else being refreshed by the water, and knowing you can never have it.

So why was hell created? We don't see it listed in the original Creation account of **Genesis 1-2**, but that's because it wasn't really needed then. God created everything to be perfect (**Genesis 1:31**), so there was no need for a place for evil to dwell. Hell was prepared as a place for the devil (the first fallen angel) and his angels to dwell (**Matthew 25:41; 2 Peter 2:4**). Hell is the place for those who have done evil, so they can face their condemnation there (**John 5:28-29; Revelation 21:8; Matthew 25:46; Matthew 13:50; Psalm 9:17**).

The devil is not necessarily in charge of hell, but he has been banished to live there forever (**Revelation 20:10**). Hell is eternal fire (**Mark 9:43**) and will destroy both body and soul (**Matthew 10:28**). We know that God cannot be and is not present there (**2**

Thessalonians 1:9). Those who dwell in hell are living in a place that is completely without God; we can only imagine the horror that that would be, since God does dwell and work in our world, even if we don't acknowledge Him.

How do we get to hell? Well, it's the opposite of how we get to heaven. We get to heaven by believing in Jesus as our savior, so we get to hell by NOT believing that. Unfortunately, the way to heaven is much narrower than the way to hell. **Matthew 7:13-14** says, "Enter through the narrow gate. For wide is the gate and broad is the road that leads to destruction, and many enter through it. But small is the gate and narrow the road that leads to life, and only a few find it."

Hell is a real place. What are you doing in your life to make sure you're going through the narrow gate to heaven and escaping the eternal torment of hell?

What the Bible Says About
Earth

In the last two sections, I wrote about what the Bible says about heaven and about hell, so earth is next on the list.

Most of the events written about in the Bible take place on earth, so for starters we could say that nearly the whole Bible says something about earth. It is the place where God's created people dwell. We are here to give Him glory and to pursue relationship with Him until the day when we can be with Him forever in heaven (or without Him forever in hell).

The main thing that the Bible says about earth is that it was created, and it says this a lot! Some examples are **Genesis 1:1, Exodus 20:11, Psalm 104:5, Job 38:4, Isaiah 42:5, Colossians 1:16-17, Jeremiah 10:12**, and **Hebrews 11:3**. Some who live on earth today adamantly refuse this fact and believe that the earth just magically appeared out of goop or something, but the Bible clearly teaches that was not the case. God created the earth as a place for His creation to dwell.

We know that the earth belongs to God, as does everything in it (**Psalm 24:1-2**). The earth is full of the knowledge of God (**Isaiah 11:9** and **Romans 1:20**), so even if a person does not have the opportunity to hear the good news about Jesus Christ, they can still see God's presence in the earth simply by living here.

But, earth is not the perfection it was once created to be. In **Genesis 1:31**, God said that all of His creation was very good. But in **Genesis 3**, humans messed it up by wanting to be like God and thinking they could actual attain that. Not only did this curse people but also the entire earth! **Genesis 3:17b-18** says, "Cursed is the ground because of you; through painful toil you will eat food from it all the days of your life. It will produce thorns and thistles for you, and you will eat the plants of the field." **Isaiah 24:4-6** echoes this fact by saying: "The earth dries up and withers, the world languishes and withers, the heavens languish with the earth. The earth is defiled by its people; they have disobeyed the laws, violated the statutes and broken the everlasting covenant. Therefore a curse consumes the earth; its people must bear their guilt. Therefore earth's inhabitants are burned up, and very few are left."

Because we messed up the earth, one day it will pass away (**Isaiah 65:17** and **Revelation 21:1**). When that day comes, all of those living on earth will be sent to either heaven or hell, depending on God's judgment of them.

God has created this earth for us to dwell in, until such time that He is ready to restore all of creation to Himself and usher in the new heaven and the new earth. What are you doing in your life to make your time on earth worthwhile, to give God glory and prepare for the day that you're no longer on this earth?

What the Bible Says About
Purgatory

Before we look into this topic of what the Bible says about purgatory, what exactly is purgatory? If you're not familiar with the Roman Catholic church, you may not have heard the word before. The catechism of the Catholic church teaches this: "All who die in God's grace, but still imperfectly purified, are indeed assured of their eternal salvation; but after death they undergo purification, so as to achieve the holiness necessary to enter the joy of heaven." Purgatory is believed to be the place where souls go to undergo this purification, before they can enter God's presence in heaven.

So what does the Bible say about this topic? The word "purgatory" doesn't actually appear in the Bible, so we'll need to look at passages that discuss the concepts.

The primary passage that Catholics use to point to purgatory is **1 Corinthians 3:15**: "If it is burned up, the builder will suffer loss but yet will be saved — even though only as one escaping through the flames." The context before this verse is Paul addressing how we are to have Jesus as our foundation, but it takes many teachers and encouragers in the body of Christ to build up one another. **1 Corinthians 3:12-15** talks about a believer's works being judged with an illustration of going through fire. If our works are of good quality, they will make it through; if they are poor quality, then they will be burned. It's the believer's work that will go through the fire, not the believer himself. Purgatory is believed to be the place where this happens - the believer's work becomes good through a purification process.

But, do we really need to be purified? **Hebrews 7:27** says, "Unlike the other high priests, he does not need to offer sacrifices day after day, first for his own sins, and then for the sins of the people. He sacrificed for their sins once for all when he offered himself." (The "he" being referred to here is Jesus.) **Romans 5:8** says, "But God demonstrates his own love for us in this: While we were still sinners, Christ died for us." **Isaiah 53:5**, prophesying about Jesus, says, "But he was pierced for our transgressions, he was crushed for our iniquities; the punishment that brought us peace was on him, and by his wounds we are healed."

Those verses all indicate that Jesus' sacrifice was enough. Once we have faith in Him as our Savior, we don't need any further purification; Jesus covered all that for us through His death on the cross. **Ephesians 2:8-9**, **1 Corinthians 15:3**, and **1 John 2:2** (among others) remind us that salvation is not anything we can accomplish by our good works, but only through the work of Jesus Christ.

According to **Revelation 21:27**, we know that nothing impure or unclean will enter heaven. We know that our sins make us impure and unclean. Every time we're disobedient to God, we separate ourselves from Him and His perfection. But that's where Jesus came in - He lived a perfect, sinless life, then died the death that we deserve. He was the perfect sacrifice, because we couldn't be.

Salvation is not about what we do; it's about what Jesus already did for us. While we all strive to live lives that give honor and glory to God, we all mess up. But when we have faith in Jesus, God sees us as He sees Jesus - completely purified, no longer in need of any further purification.

So what does the Bible say about purgatory? Nothing - it's not needed! Jesus took care of everything for us.

What the Bible Says About
War

"You shall not murder" (**Exodus 20:13**). But yet, there are numerous times that God commands the Israelites to go to war, which results in the killing of often thousands of people. How do we reconcile these? What does the Bible really say about war?

Part of the distinction lies in the definition. The Hebrew word used for "murder" in the Ten Commandments has the idea of a premeditated killing of that specific person with malice. We see in **Exodus 21:12-17** (the very next chapter after the Ten Commandments) that there are some crimes that God commanded the death penalty for under Old Testament law, including kidnapping, attacking one's parents, or even cursing one's parents! So we see that God is not necessarily against the taking of all life, but it depends on the circumstances.

There are many wars and battles recorded in the Old Testament, primarily between Israel and the pagan peoples who surrounded them, and many of these were ordered by God. We even see a civil war between the Israelite tribe of Benjamin and the rest of Israel in **Judges 20**, that was sanctioned by God! God does not change, so if God was okay with war in the Old Testament, then He still is today. In fact, we know from **Revelation 14:14-20** and **Revelation 19:11-21** that battles at the end of the world will be gory and violent.

The fact of the matter is that while humans are sinful, God's natural law is in place on this earth. Sometimes, war is necessary for punishments to be carried out according to that natural law. There are times that God uses war to stop a greater evil. For example, what would have happened in Nazi Germany in the 1940s if World War II had not happened? That war defeated Hitler and stopped the Holocaust. While millions of Jews did lose their lives, millions more may have died had things been left unchecked. War is a bad thing, but human sinfulness can be even worse.

What the Bible tells us about war needs to be interpreted in the context of God's character. While He is a loving God, He is also a just God. We know from **Romans 3:9-20** that all human beings are sinful, and we deserve punishment. We know that all have sinned and fall short of the glory of God (**Romans 3:23**), and the wages of sin is death (**Romans 6:23**) - which could mean war, depending on the circumstances and what God decides is just.

Based on what we see in the Bible, we can't say that war is right in every circumstance, and we can't say that it is wrong in every circumstance. What we can say is that the God who is sovereign will allow war when necessary and prevent it when not. Trust the God who created the universe to take care of His people on earth as He sees fit.

What the Bible Says About
Sex Before Marriage

If you're a teenager or young adult who is a follower of Jesus, my guess is that this question has crossed your mind at least once: what does the Bible really say about having sex before marriage? Hopefully this writing will help answer that question for you.

We at Worldview Warriors wrote on this topic previously during 2014 when we answered many tough questions. You can search for my post on "What is Fornication?" at our blog website, WorldviewWarriors.org/Blog. As I wrote in that post, sexual sin is inside one's own body, rather than an external sin, so in that situation we are not honoring God with our bodies. You can find more on this in **1 Corinthians 6:13-20**. When we are followers of Jesus, we are united with Him and the Spirit, so sexual sin is defiling the temple of the Holy Spirit.

The apostle Paul gives some additional advice regarding sex in **1 Corinthians 7:2** and **7:8-9**. He encourages unmarried men and women to refrain from having sex. But being a man himself he realizes this may be difficult, so if you're not able to control yourself, then just get married! That may seem crass to us in the 21ˢᵗ century, but if you're willing to unite yourself with another human being in that intimate way (**Genesis 2:24**), then you should be willing to spend the rest of your life with them.

So according to the Bible, having sex with anyone other than your spouse is considered to be sexual immorality. What does the Bible say about sexual immorality? A lot! Check out these passages:

"It is my judgment, therefore, that we should not make it difficult for the Gentiles who are turning to God. Instead we should write to them, telling them to abstain from food polluted by idols, from sexual immorality, from the meat of strangled animals and from blood." (**Acts 15:19-20**)

"It is actually reported that there is sexual immorality among you, and of a kind that even pagans do not tolerate: A man is sleeping with his father's wife." (**1 Corinthians 5:1**)

"We should not commit sexual immorality, as some of them did — and in one day twenty-three thousand of them died." (**1 Corinthians 10:8**)

"I am afraid that when I come again my God will humble me before you, and I will be grieved over many who have sinned earlier and have not repented of the impurity, sexual sin and debauchery in which they have indulged." (**2 Corinthians 12:21**)

"The acts of the flesh are obvious: sexual immorality, impurity and debauchery; idolatry and witchcraft; hatred, discord, jealousy, fits of rage, selfish ambition, dissensions, factions and envy; drunkenness, orgies, and the like. I warn you, as I did before, that those who live like this will not inherit the kingdom of God." (**Galatians 5:19-21**)

"But among you there must not be even a hint of sexual immorality, or of any kind of impurity, or of greed, because these are improper for God's holy people." (**Ephesians 5:3**)

"Put to death, therefore, whatever belongs to your earthly nature: sexual immorality, impurity, lust, evil desires and greed, which is idolatry." (**Colossians 3:5**)

"It is God's will that you should be sanctified: that you should avoid sexual immorality; that each of you should learn to control your own body in a way that is holy and honorable, not in passionate lust like the pagans, who do not know God;" (**1 Thessalonians 4:3-5**)

"In a similar way, Sodom and Gomorrah and the surrounding towns gave themselves up to sexual immorality and perversion. They serve as an example of those who suffer the punishment of eternal fire." (**Jude 7**)

"Marriage should be honored by all, and the marriage bed kept pure, for God will judge the adulterer and all the sexually immoral." (**Hebrews 13:4**)

If those aren't enough for you I could probably find a few more, but those should make it clear: sexual immorality is sin in God's eyes. There is no situation in which it is considered right.

From a practical viewpoint, think about the benefits of not having sex outside of marriage: fewer sexually transmitted diseases, significantly less abortions and unwanted pregnancies, and more children growing up in households where both parents are present. Abstinence not only honors God, but it's practical as well.

Anyone who is a follower of Jesus should desire to honor God with our whole lives - including all our actions and what we do with our bodies. The Bible is pretty clear that this is God's position, so it should be our position as well when we are following Him.

What the Bible Says About
Sex After Marriage

In the last section, I wrote on what the Bible says about sex before marriage, so that begs the question: what about sex after marriage?

Before answering this question, we first need to establish what marriage is. Marriage is between one man and one woman. It can't be redefined to be anything else, because it was instituted by God. The marriage relationship should be like that of God and the church. For more on those topics, check out blog posts from February 2014 on the Worldview Warriors Blog.

Hebrews 13:4 talks about sex both before and after marriage: "Marriage should be honored by all, and the marriage bed kept pure, for God will judge the adulterer and all the sexually immoral." Keeping the marriage bed pure means that sex will only happen between a husband and wife. Once two people have intercourse, they become one flesh (**Genesis 2:24**).

The apostle Paul gives advice to married couples in **1 Corinthians 7**. **Verses 3-4** say, "The husband should fulfill his marital duty to his wife, and likewise the wife to her husband. The wife does not have authority over her own body but yields it to her husband. In the same way, the husband does not have authority over his own body but yields it to his wife." Once a couple is married, Paul commands them to stay married, because they are already united as one flesh, in **verses 10-11**: "To the married I give this command (not I, but the Lord): A wife must not separate from her husband. But if she does, she must remain unmarried or else be reconciled to her husband. And a husband must not divorce his wife."

Similarly, the Bible tells us that sex after marriage should not include adultery (sex with someone other than your spouse) or prostitution.

"You shall not commit adultery." (**Exodus 20:14**)

"Do you not know that your bodies are members of Christ himself? Shall I then take the members of Christ and unite them with a prostitute? Never! Do you not know that he who unites himself with a prostitute is one with her in body? For it is said, "The two will become one flesh." But whoever is united with the Lord is one with him in spirit." (**1 Corinthians 6:15-17**)

"You have heard that it was said, 'You shall not commit adultery.' But I tell you that anyone who looks at a woman lustfully has already committed adultery with her in his heart." (**Matthew 5:27-28**)

Regarding the details of sex between a husband and wife within the context of marriage, the Bible is not very specific. But the general guideline to follow is to determine whether that particular act is good, beneficial, and loving. In **1 Corinthians 6:12**, Paul says, "'I have the right to do anything,' you say — but not everything is beneficial. 'I have the right to do anything' — but I will not be mastered by anything." While the context of this passage is not specifically related to sex, the concept still applies. Just because you can do something doesn't necessarily mean it's good or beneficial. That's where discernment and discussion between the husband and wife needs to take place.

So what does the Bible say? While sex before (or outside of) marriage is condemned as sin by the Bible, sex after and in the context of marriage is encouraged.

What the Bible Says About
Sports

Anyone who knows me knows that I am not a sports fan. I never have been, and I'm pretty sure I never will be. If I had to choose a favorite sport it would be baseball, simply because I know the most about it, having gone to numerous baseball games with my baseball-fan family growing up. While I will attend an occasional game as a social event, it's not something I often choose to do in my free time.

So the question here is what does the Bible say about sports? There are a number of sports metaphors in the Bible. For example, **Philippians 3:13b-14** says, "But one thing I do: Forgetting what is behind and straining toward what is ahead, I press on toward the goal to win the prize for which God has called me heavenward in Christ Jesus."

1 Corinthians 9:24-27 uses sports metaphors to explain having self-discipline in our spiritual life: "Do you not know that in a race all the runners run, but only one gets the prize? Run in such a way as to get the prize. Everyone who competes in the games goes into strict training. They do it to get a crown that will not last, but we do it to get a crown that will last forever. Therefore I do not run like someone running aimlessly; I do not fight like a boxer beating the air. No, I strike a blow to my body and make it my slave so that after I have preached to others, I myself will not be disqualified for the prize."

1 Timothy 4:8 takes that one step farther, saying, "For physical training is of some value, but godliness has value for all things, holding promise for both the present life and the life to come."

When the apostle Paul was nearing the end of his life, he compared it to the end of a race in **2 Timothy 4:7-8**: "I have fought the good fight, I have finished the race, I have kept the faith. Now there is in store for me the crown of righteousness, which the Lord, the righteous Judge, will award to me on that day—and not only to me, but also to all who have longed for his appearing."

While the Bible does not mention specifics for every sporting situation, we need to look at its overall meaning and realize that whatever we are doing (whether it be playing sports, watching sports, or some other activity), we should be good witnesses of our faith and the God we serve in everything. We see this in **1 Peter 3:15**, **Matthew 5:14-16**, and **1 Corinthians 10:31**.

We also need to be cautious against sinning within the context of sports. The main cautions we get from the Bible that would apply to sports are pride and idolatry.

We can easily become prideful when either we are particularly good at a certain sport, or when our favorite team is doing very well. There are many verses in Proverbs that talk about the negative effects of pride, but here are a couple. **Proverbs 11:2** says, "When pride comes, then comes disgrace, but with humility comes wisdom." **Proverbs 27:2** says, "Let someone else praise you, and not your own mouth; an outsider, and not your own lips." When we boast in ourselves and our own accomplishments, we are being prideful. Sports frequently bring attention to the accomplishments of the individual, rather than giving glory to God.

Idolatry is addressed in **Matthew 22:37-38**: "Jesus replied: 'Love the Lord your God with all your heart and with all your soul and with all your mind.' This is the first and greatest commandment." If we put anything else as a higher priority in life than God, then we are loving that thing and not loving God with our whole heart. **1 John 5:21** is pretty self-explanatory: "Dear children, keep yourselves from idols." Anything that we worship more than we worship God is an idol in our lives.

How can you tell if sports are an idol in your life? If you play sports, do you make games or practice a priority over spending time with

God in your life? If you watch sports, can you name all the players on your favorite team, but not the books of the Bible? Does watching sports get in the way of your time spent worshiping God? Do you wish the pastor would preach a shorter sermon on Sundays so you can get home in time for kickoff? Consider how you spend your time and where your priorities are at.

There is nothing inherently sinful about sports according to what the Bible says, but we should be cautioned that sports of any sort (or anything else for that matter) are not to be a higher priority in our lives than the God who created us with the abilities and passions He has given us.

What the Bible Says About
Money

Money: we either love it or hate it, feel like we have plenty of it or never enough. Even when we really do have enough, we always seem to want more. Money and how we handle it has been an issue in society for hundreds of years, which is why we see the topic a lot in the Bible. There are hundreds of verses either specifically or loosely related to money! That's a bit much to list in this writing, but we'll go over some of the highlights of what the Bible says about money.

The Bible talks about money in general in a number of verses. Perhaps the most often-quoted one is at the end of the passage in **1 Timothy 6:7-10**: "For we brought nothing into the world, and we can take nothing out of it. But if we have food and clothing, we will be content with that. Those who want to get rich fall into temptation and a trap and into many foolish and harmful desires that plunge people into ruin and destruction. For the love of money is a root of all kinds of evil. Some people, eager for money, have wandered from the faith and pierced themselves with many griefs." You can't take money with you, and if you love money more than you love God, it will get you into all kinds of evil.

Similarly, in **Matthew 6:24**, we see that we can't serve both God and money. We can't focus our lives around money and still be focused on God; our focus needs to be on one or the other (ideally God, of course). The story of the rich young ruler in **Matthew 19:16-24** that provides the context for this verse illustrates that truth. We know that wherever our heart is - whether with our money / possessions or with God - that is where our treasure is (**Matthew 6:21**). If our heart is following money and getting more stuff in this world, then that's the treasure we're storing up for ourselves: that which we can't take with us. But if our heart is following after God, then we're earning a treasure that will bless us for all eternity.

There are numerous verses in Proverbs that talk about wealth and money. For example, **Proverbs 11:4** says, "Wealth is worthless in the day of wrath, but righteousness delivers from death." **Proverbs 23:4-5** says, "Do not wear yourself out to get rich; do not trust your own cleverness. Cast but a glance at riches, and they are gone, for they will surely sprout wings and fly off to the sky like an eagle."

Much of the book of Ecclesiastes is about what actually has value in life, and **Ecclesiastes 5:8-20** talks about riches specifically. **Verse 10** sums it up: "Whoever loves money never has enough; whoever loves wealth is never satisfied with their income. This too is meaningless."

Another money-related topic in the Bible is giving, whether giving money to others, to the church, or to other organizations that spread God's Kingdom. **2 Corinthians 9:7** says, "Each of you should give what you have decided in your heart to give, not reluctantly or under compulsion, for God loves a cheerful giver." **Luke 6:32-35** talks about lending to others who are genuinely in need, while not expecting repayment, along with the idea of loving your enemies. **Proverbs 22:9** says, "The generous will themselves be blessed, for they share their food with the poor." **Matthew 6:2-4** gives further instruction on how to give to the poor, specifically that we don't make a big deal about it, since we're just being obedient to God and should not be prideful in the matter.

Yet another money issue discussed in the Bible is the sin of greed - wanting money or possessions that we do not have, and likely don't even need. "Then [Jesus] said to them, 'Watch out! Be on your guard against all kinds of greed; life does not consist in an abundance of possessions'" (**Luke 12:15**). "What good is it for someone to gain the whole world, yet forfeit their soul?" (**Mark 8:36**). **Ephesians 5:5** warns us that those who are greedy will not inherit God's Kingdom: "For of this you can be sure: No immoral, impure or greedy person—such a person is an idolater—has any inheritance in the kingdom of Christ and of God."

Debt is also discussed in the Bible. Much of **Proverbs 22** talks about money, and **verse 7** specifically deals with the position we put ourselves in when we go into debt: "The rich rule over the poor, and the borrower is slave to the lender." **Verses 26-27** warn about going into debt if you can't afford to pay it back: "Do not be one who shakes hands in pledge or puts up security for debts; if you lack the means to pay, your very bed will be snatched from under you." Biblically, the only debt we should have in our lives is a debt of loving each other: "Let no debt remain outstanding, except the continuing debt to love one another, for whoever loves others has fulfilled the law" (**Romans 13:8**).

Finally, we're encouraged in Scripture to not worry about money, because God will provide for our needs. **Matthew 6:25-33** is a great passage that speaks about this, ending with telling us what we should seek instead: God's Kingdom and His righteousness. When we do that with our whole hearts, we don't have to worry about anything! God can and will take care of us when we are obedient to Him in doing His work: "And my God will meet all your needs according to the riches of his glory in Christ Jesus." (**Philippians 4:19**). This has also been promised by God since Old Testament times, as it says in **Deuteronomy 8:18**: "But remember the Lord your God, for it is he who gives you the ability to produce wealth, and so confirms his covenant, which he swore to your ancestors, as it is today." If we delight in the Lord, He will give us the desires of our hearts (**Psalm 37:4**), and we will be content with what we have.

God doesn't want us to struggle with the issue of money. If we are following His plan for our lives and being obedient to what He wants us to do, money will not be an issue for us. There are many resources available online to help you manage your money in a Biblical way.

"And God is able to bless you abundantly, so that in all things at all times, having all that you need, you will abound in every good work." (**2 Corinthians 9:8**)

What the Bible Says About
Work

After the previous section about what the Bible says about money, writing on what the Bible says about work seems like a natural follow up. Many people have a particular job simply for the money and not necessarily because they have a passion for that type of work. But is that the attitude we should have? What does the Bible say?

God created work in the Garden of Eden, even before mankind fell into sin. **Genesis 2:15** says, "The Lord God took the man and put him in the Garden of Eden to work it and take care of it." One of Adam's purposes was to work in taking care of the garden. But without sin in the world, that work would have been completely enjoyable!

However, after sin, work got significantly worse. "To Adam he said, 'Because you listened to your wife and ate fruit from the tree about which I commanded you, 'You must not eat from it.' Cursed is the ground because of you; through painful toil you will eat food from it all the days of your life. It will produce thorns and thistles for you, and you will eat the plants of the field. By the sweat of your brow you will eat your food until you return to the ground, since from it you were taken; for dust you are and to dust you will return.'" (**Genesis 3:17-19**)

Because of sin, work is not always a fun thing for us humans, although we were created to do work - God's work. God didn't create us to sit around and be lazy all day (more on that in the next section), but to work at what He has called us to do, to accomplish His purposes. That doesn't mean we're all called to full-time vocational ministry, but whatever we are doing in life we should do in a way that glorifies God.

"Whatever you do, work at it with all your heart, as working for the Lord, not for human masters." (**Colossians 3:23**)

"So whether you eat or drink or whatever you do, do it all for the glory of God." (**1 Corinthians 10:31**)

"Commit to the Lord whatever you do, and he will establish your plans." (**Proverbs 16:3**)

We know that when we work hard, we will profit from it in some way. "Those who work their land will have abundant food, but those who chase fantasies have no sense" (**Proverbs 12:11**).

"All hard work brings a profit, but mere talk leads only to poverty" (**Proverbs 14:23**).

We should set an example to those around us through working hard, doing our tasks well, and working with integrity in all that we do. **Titus 2:7-8** says, "In everything set them an example by doing what is good. In your teaching show integrity, seriousness and soundness of speech that cannot be condemned, so that those who oppose you may be ashamed because they have nothing bad to say about us." **Matthew 5:16** says, "In the same way, let your light shine before others, that they may see your good deeds and glorify your Father in heaven."

One of the most important things to remember about work is that we will reap what we sow. If you sow good things such as working well, you will reap good things; if you sow bad things such as doing as little as you can and with a bad attitude, you will reap bad things such as punishment or no longer having that job. **Galatians 6:7-10** says, "Do not be deceived: God cannot be mocked. A man reaps what he sows. Whoever sows to please their flesh, from the flesh will reap destruction; whoever sows to please the Spirit, from the Spirit will reap eternal life. Let us not become weary in doing good, for at the proper time we will reap a harvest if we do not give up. Therefore, as we have opportunity, let us do good to all people, especially to those who belong to the family of believers."

Ephesians 4:28 encourages us to work to get what we need, rather than through stealing or other dishonest methods: "Anyone who has been stealing must steal no longer, but must work, doing something useful with their own hands, that they may have something to share with those in need." Work makes us productive members of society, helping those around us.

Finally, we are commanded to do what God instructs us to do, whatever kind of work that might be. James 2:14-26 tells us that without works (doing what God instructs us), our faith is dead. James 1:22 says that we should not just listen to God's Word but do what it says.

The Bible tells us that work is a good thing, created by God and for mankind to do to fulfill God's purposes. We work to serve and glorify God and to help those around us, so that in all things we might honor the God who created us. I encourage you to make that your attitude every day.

What the Bible Says About
Laziness

In the last section, I wrote about what the Bible says about work, so here we're looking at the opposite side of that: what the Bible says about laziness. Google defines laziness as, "the quality of being unwilling to work or use energy; idleness." So being lazy is the opposite of being willing to work.

The book of Proverbs has a lot of references to a lazy or idle person! I'll list just a few here, since there are so many.

"Lazy hands make for poverty, but diligent hands bring wealth." (**Proverbs 10:4**)

"Diligent hands will rule, but laziness ends in forced labor." (**Proverbs 12:24**)

"The lazy do not roast any game, but the diligent feed on the riches of the hunt." (**Proverbs 12:27**)

"A sluggard's appetite is never filled, but the desires of the diligent are fully satisfied." (**Proverbs 13:4**)

"One who is slack in his work is brother to one who destroys." (**Proverbs 18:9**)

Laziness is mentioned in other parts of the Bible, too. Paul talks about it pretty thoroughly in **2 Thessalonians 3:6-13**. He delivers a pretty severe warning against those who are idle and lazy. He shares how he works for a living rather than simply living off what others provide, so that he can be a model for them to imitate. He commands the people of Thessalonica to earn what they receive, work for a living, and not be lazy.

Having a life of laziness means that one would not provide for themselves or their own family. Paul warns against this in **1 Timothy 5:8**: "Anyone who does not provide for their relatives, and especially for their own household, has denied the faith and is worse than an unbeliever." Of course there are situations where a person is physically unable to do certain jobs for a living and provide for themselves in this way, but if a person is capable of doing anything to provide for themselves and their family (whether it's a paying income or just bettering society), then they should do that, rather than living a life of laziness.

Note that laziness is different from rest. God modeled (**Genesis 2:2-3**) then commanded (**Exodus 20:8-11**) that we all honor His example and rest from our work one day a week. That is not laziness, but fulfilling what God has commanded us to do. Times of rest are required for our bodies to recharge and be able to do the work that God has called us to do.

So, what the Bible says about laziness is basically that it's the opposite of working. God created work and we are called to do it; laziness is going against what God has designed for us as human beings.

What the Bible Says About
Who God Is

When I first began pondering this topic, I wanted to simply write, "See: entire Bible." That's true, you know? The whole of the Bible is God revealing Himself and His character to us as His creation. We cannot understand Him fully, but we have 66 books that give us a really good idea of who He is. So, the entire Bible - all the way from Genesis to Revelation - tells us something about God's character.

But to summarize it a bit more for you, let's start at the beginning. **Genesis 1:1** says, "In the beginning, God created the heavens and the earth." God is the creator; He is the one who made us and everything that we see. He created life out of nothing! For more on that, check out Worldview Warriors blog posts by Steve Risner, as he has spent much time refuting evolutionary theory with creation as described in the Bible.

God further reveals His identity in the story of Moses. When God was calling Moses to lead the people of Israel out of Egypt, Moses asked for God's name to tell Pharaoh. In **Exodus 3:14**, "God said to Moses, 'I am who I am. This is what you are to say to the Israelites: 'I am has sent me to you.'" Knowing a person's name tell us a part of their identity; the same goes with God. God is the I AM - He has no beginning and no end, He just is.

When Jesus came down to this world in human form, in His earthly ministry, He closely linked Himself with the Father. In the gospel of John, there are seven "I am" statements that Jesus made:

John 6:35: "Then Jesus declared, 'I am the bread of life. Whoever comes to me will never go hungry, and whoever believes in me will never be thirsty.'"

John 8:12: "When Jesus spoke again to the people, he said, 'I am the light of the world. Whoever follows me will never walk in darkness, but will have the light of life.'"

John 10:9: "I am the gate; whoever enters through me will be saved. They will come in and go out, and find pasture."

John 10:11: "I am the good shepherd. The good shepherd lays down his life for the sheep."

John 11:25: "Jesus said to her, 'I am the resurrection and the life. The one who believes in me will live, even though they die.'"

John 14:6: "Jesus answered, 'I am the way and the truth and the life.'"

John 15:1: "I am the true vine, and my Father is the gardener."

I encourage you to read the context around each of those passages to get a better idea of who Jesus is. In using the phrase "I am" in the way that He did, Jesus was linking Himself with God the Father and proving that He, too, was God in the flesh.

We see who God is further in the passage of **John 1:1-18**. The Word referred to in that passage is Jesus. In the beginning was Jesus, and Jesus was with God, and Jesus was God. He was with God in the beginning. God is eternal; He is eternal as the Father, the Son, and the Holy Spirit.

The Bible is the primary way we know who God is, how He relates to us, and how we should relate to Him. These passages I mentioned are just a very small sampling of the entire Scripture, that as a whole give us the best description of a God who is both knowable and unknowable, personal and unimaginable.

That right there is the best gift we could ever receive!

What the Bible Says About
Anger

While we should start off every day on a positive note, the reality is that sin is in this world. People (maybe even you) are living with anger in their lives for whatever reason. Maybe you're angry at a person for a way they have wronged you. Maybe you're angry at the circumstances of your life, that may or may not be a result of your choices. Maybe you're angry at yourself for the choices you've made. But whatever the reason, keep reading to see what the Bible says about anger - and maybe these verses will help you live on a more positive note.

Perhaps you've heard of the idea of "righteous anger" - anger that is not considered sin, because it is indignation that is intended to spur us on to solve the problems of the world. An example of righteous anger would be anger over an injustice in the world, such as orphans being oppressed, or a government withholding food or basic necessities from its people. When we see in the Bible that God gets angry or has wrath, that's the type of anger He has, because God does not sin. **Psalm 7:11** says, "God is a righteous judge, a God who displays his wrath every day." **Mark 3:5** (speaking about Jesus, who is God, healing a man on the Sabbath) says, "He looked around at them in anger and, deeply distressed at their stubborn hearts, said to the man, 'Stretch out your hand.' He stretched it out, and his hand was completely restored."

Believers receive a caution regarding our anger in **Ephesians 4:26-27**: "'In your anger do not sin': Do not let the sun go down while you are still angry, and do not give the devil a foothold." There is a VERY fine line between righteous anger and anger that is sinful, and we need to be extremely cautious not to cross that line into anger. But, most of the time, the anger that we as humans have is sinful. When we express our anger in unhealthy ways, such as getting mad at whoever caused it, that's sinful. **Proverbs 29:11** explains that, "Fools give full vent to their rage, but the wise bring calm in the end."

What causes anger? **James 4:1-6** gives a good explanation: "What causes fights and quarrels among you? Don't they come from your desires that battle within you? You desire but do not have, so you kill. You covet but you cannot get what you want, so you quarrel and fight. You do not have because you do not ask God. When you ask, you do not receive, because you ask with wrong motives, that you may spend what you get on your pleasures. You adulterous people, don't you know that friendship with the world means enmity against God? Therefore, anyone who chooses to be a friend of the world becomes an enemy of God. Or do you think Scripture says without reason that he jealously longs for the spirit he has caused to dwell in us? But he gives us more grace. That is why Scripture says: 'God opposes the proud but shows favor to the humble.'"

So what can we do when we do get angry? We should recognize and admit our anger and confess it to God. **Proverbs 28:13** says, "Whoever conceals their sins does not prosper, but the one who confesses and renounces them finds mercy." We should confess our sin both to God and to the person(s) with whom we are angry.

We can also handle our anger Biblically by doing good instead of retaliating. We see this in **Romans 12:21**: "Do not be overcome by evil, but overcome evil with good." We also see Jesus explaining this further in **Matthew 5:43-48**, that we are to love our enemies (those who cause us to be angry). **Proverbs 19:11** says, "A person's wisdom yields patience; it is to one's glory to overlook an offense."

We are also commanded to live at peace with everyone as best as we are able (**Romans 12:18**), so that our actions do not cause others to become angry. **Proverbs 15:1** says, "A gentle answer turns away wrath, but a harsh word stirs up anger."

The best advice regarding anger is to simply not get angry in the first place, though of course that is easier said than done. **Psalm 37:8-9** says, "Refrain from anger and turn from wrath; do not fret—

it leads only to evil. For those who are evil will be destroyed, but those who hope in the Lord will inherit the land." **Ecclesiastes 7:9** says, "Do not be quickly provoked in your spirit, for anger resides in the lap of fools."

To sum it up: "My dear brothers and sisters, take note of this: Everyone should be quick to listen, slow to speak and slow to become angry, because human anger does not produce the righteousness that God desires." (**James 1:19-20**).

What the Bible Says About
Bitterness

In the last section, I wrote on what the Bible says about anger. This section's topic is closely related to that: what the Bible says about bitterness.

What's the difference between anger and bitterness? Generally speaking, anger is the reaction to a hurt that is presently going on, whereas bitterness is how we feel about past hurts that we can't (or won't) let go of. Anger can often go away quickly, while bitterness is a lingering emotion. We can control our anger and how we react to it, but when we let bitterness take hold of us, it controls us. We often act on our anger, but bitterness generally festers more quietly.

So what does the Bible say about bitterness? Primarily, it tells us to get rid of it. **Ephesians 4:31-32** says, "Get rid of all bitterness, rage and anger, brawling and slander, along with every form of malice. Be kind and compassionate to one another, forgiving each other, just as in Christ God forgave you." Note how bitterness is linked to the need for forgiveness; bitterness happens when someone angers us and we don't forgive them. Jesus tells us how many times we should forgive someone in **Matthew 18:21-22**: essentially, as many times as they wrong us.

We see that if we hold on to bitterness and don't forgive those who have wronged us, God will not forgive us. Jesus tells us about this in **Matthew 6:14-15**, **Mark 11:25**, and **Luke 17:3-4**.

Note that in **1 Corinthians 13:4-6**, we see that love keeps no record of wrongs. Keeping track of how someone has wronged you generally leads to bitterness, because you're holding onto the times they have made you angry.

To keep bitterness out of your life, follow the words given to us in **Hebrews 12:14-15**: "Make every effort to live in peace with everyone and to be holy; without holiness no one will see the Lord. See to it that no one falls short of the grace of God and that no bitter root grows up to cause trouble and defile many." Be on guard against the danger that bitterness can have on your life; if left untreated and unforgiven, it will lead you and others astray from God's Word.

What the Bible Says About
Aliens from Another Planet

And now for something kind of different... what does the Bible say about aliens from another planet? When I first read that topic, my response was that I couldn't think of a single Bible passage that talks about aliens. But let's dig into it and see what the Bible tells us on this topic.

A key part of answering this question lies in defining what "aliens" are. Generally speaking, aliens are defined as beings similar to humans - capable of making decisions, having intelligence, and having emotions. Aliens are not algae, bacteria, single-celled organisms, or anything like that.

We know from **Genesis 1-2** that God created the entire universe - including earth, of course, and all the other planets. God created the earth before He created the sun, moon, or the stars. God created the earth to be inhabited by humans (**Isaiah 45:18**). Humans are still exploring the vastness of the universe, but of all the planets we have been able to send technology to, none of them are capable of supporting life as the earth is. We know that when God created humans, he put them on earth. There is no evidence in the creation account that God did the same thing anywhere else in the universe.

Genesis 1:31 tells us that, "God saw all that he had made, and it was very good." At the time of Creation, before mankind sinned, EVERYTHING that God had made was good - including the entire universe and all other planets. **Romans 8:19-22** tells us that the whole creation fell when humans sinned and has been suffering ever since, so if there were aliens on another planet, they would be suffering as well. We know that Jesus Christ came to earth to die once and for all (**Hebrews 7:27**) to save mankind from our sins. He didn't do this on any other planet, but on earth. So if God had created aliens elsewhere, they would be left to suffer in their sin without even the hope of a savior; would a loving God do that? I'd venture to say no.

The Bible gives us no reason to believe that there are aliens on any other planets in the universe. So what does the Bible say about aliens from other planets? Nothing, because they don't exist.

What the Bible Says About
Dinosaurs

Dinosaurs have gone in and out of popularity in our culture, often depending on what movies are popular at the time. Dinosaurs fascinate us because they aren't alive today, but we have evidence that they existed, primarily in the fossil record.

The word "dinosaur" is not in the Bible at all, since that word was developed in 1841 by Sir Richard Owen. It comes from the Greek words "deinos" (meaning terrible or monstrous) and "sauros" (meaning lizard). So there is no ancient Hebrew or Greek word that literally means dinosaur.

So are dinosaurs mentioned specifically in the Bible? One passage that is often pointed to for dinosaurs is **Job 40-41**. **Job 40:15-24** references "behemoth." The word "behemoth" is a literal transliteration from the Hebrew; that's how the Hebrew word would be pronounced. Scholars disagree about its meaning; it could mean hippopotamus, or elephant, or a very large creature. The Hebrew word is very similar to the one used in **Genesis 1:24-25** that's often translated as "cattle" or "livestock." But from the description in the book of Job, the Behemoth definitely sounds like how we would picture dinosaurs.

In **Job 41**, the Leviathan is another creature that we aren't really sure what it is. Its description again makes it sound like how we would picture dinosaurs. Leviathan is also mentioned in **Psalm 74:14**, **Psalm 104:25-26**, and **Isaiah 27:1**.

So if these creatures were around in Biblical times, where are they now? The most likely explanation is that they were wiped out in the flood of **Genesis 6-7**. Other than the fossils that have been discovered, we have little way of knowing what animals were wiped out in that great flood approximately 4500 years ago. We know from the fossils that dinosaurs were once alive, so they were created by God, but the Bible is pretty quiet on the subject.

Fortunately, the issue of details surrounding dinosaurs is not a matter of life and death; our salvation is not dependent on dinosaurs but rather on our faith in Jesus and His saving death and resurrection on the cross for us. What we believe regarding dinosaurs is irrelevant on that matter, which is why it's okay that the Bible doesn't share much on that specific topic; it just doesn't really matter.

What the Bible Says About
Dreams and Visions

The topic for this section is what the Bible says about dreams and visions. Yes, that does mean dreams like the kind you may have when you fall asleep at night. Visions are often prophetic in nature, meaning they tell of things yet to come.

The primary thing we see in the Bible on this topic is that God does sometimes reveal things to His people through dreams and visions. A few examples of this are in **Genesis 37:5-10, 1 Kings 3:5-15, Daniel chapter 2** and **chapter 7, Matthew 1:20, Matthew 2:13 and 19, Acts 10:9-16**, and **Acts 16:9**. There are many more examples beyond this as well.

But just because we see or experience something in a dream does not mean it's from God. **Jeremiah 23:25-27** warns of this in that some dreams are deceptive.

Does God communicate with us today through dreams and visions? Perhaps at times He does, but we need to make sure that any message we think we're receiving from God lines up with the Scriptures. We know that all Scripture was given to us by God (**2 Timothy 3:16-17**), and we should test whatever we think may (or may not) be from God (**1 John 4:1-3**).

Hebrews 1:1-2 tells us that the primary way God communicates to us today is through His Son, but that doesn't rule out that He would occasionally use dreams or visions. We do see in **Joel 2:28** and **Acts 2:17** that in the "last days" that people will have dreams and visions. Are the last days happening right now? Possibly; no one knows for sure.

Any dreams or visions you have that might be spiritual or prophetic in nature should always be checked against what we know to be true - God's Word.

What the Bible Says About
Physical Healing

We all deal with physical sickness in our lives, whether we are sick ourselves or we have a loved one with an illness. Some sickness like the common cold or the flu may stick around for a few days or a week, and then our body fights it and we're all better. Other times, as with cancer, it's more of a struggle that our body may not win. Some sickness can be lived with for a lifetime, while others cut that life short. But we all experience and deal with sickness in some way.

When we are dealing with sickness, what do we want? Healing. Sometimes the body can heal itself because of the amazing way that God has created our bodies to function. Other times medication can help speed the process along. But when we are sick, we want to be healed. So what does the Bible say about physical healing?

First, before talking about healing, we have to know where our sicknesses came from. Before mankind sinned, there was no sickness, so there was no need for healing! When mankind disobeyed God in **Genesis 3**, the perfect world became broken. The once-perfect bodies that God had created would now have illnesses and difficulties as they got older and worn out.

Psalm 41:1-3 says, "Blessed are those who have regard for the weak; the Lord delivers them in times of trouble. The Lord protects and preserves them—they are counted among the blessed in the land—he does not give them over to the desire of their foes. The Lord sustains them on their sickbed and restores them from their bed of illness." That passage seems to promise physical healing for all those "who have regard for the weak," right? Similarly, **Psalm 103:2-3** says, "Praise the Lord, my soul, and forget not all his benefits—who forgives all your sins and heals all your diseases."

If these are promises from God that we will be healed, why doesn't everyone experience physical healing in this life? While we live in this sinful world, we'll have to deal with sin and brokenness, including physical sickness. Note that those passages don't indicate WHEN God will heal us. **1 Peter 5:10** says, "And the God of all grace, who called you to his eternal glory in Christ, after you have suffered a little while, will himself restore you and make you strong, firm and steadfast." We know from **Revelation 21:4** that when we as believers join Jesus in heaven, there will be no more sickness: "There will be no more death or mourning or crying or pain."

However, the Bible does give many examples of physical ailments being healed while on this earth, primarily as Jesus healed many people during His earthly ministry. **Matthew 9:35** says, "Jesus went through all the towns and villages, teaching in their synagogues, proclaiming the good news of the kingdom and healing every disease and sickness." To quote some specific examples, Jesus healed the woman who had bled for 12 years (**Matthew 9:20-22**), 10 lepers (**Luke 17:11-19**), a paralyzed man (**Mark 2:1-12**), a blind man (**John 9:1-7**), and a crippled woman (**Luke 13:10-13**), just to name a few. After Jesus was raised from the dead and ascended into heaven, His disciples were able to perform some acts of physical healing as well, including the one described in **Acts 3:1-8**.

God may or may not grant us physical healing of our ailments today, depending on what lines up with His will. We can always ask Him in prayer for the healing that we desire, though His answer may or may not be what we want to hear. We can trust that God hears our prayers, and if His will is to heal our physical diseases, then we will be healed. Regardless of our status of physical healing, as followers of Christ, we are called to glorify God in all that we do!

What the Bible Says About
Miracles

What is a miracle? Google defines it as, "a surprising and welcome event that is not explicable by natural or scientific laws and is therefore considered to be the work of a divine agency" and as "a highly improbable or extraordinary event, development, or accomplishment that brings very welcome consequences." Essentially, miracles are things that we really can't explain logically; they may astound us and be almost unbelievable. Miracles are generally considered to be good things.

One example that we in Worldview Warriors have experienced was the healing of our president, Jason DeZurik. On December 15, 2017, Jason had a life-threatening stroke and very nearly died. Within 24 hours, he was moving all his extremities, talking well, and even joking! Within just over a week, he was out of the ICU. In less than 2 weeks after the stroke, he was back home. He was back to mostly normal life in just a few months. His healing has been nothing short of miraculous!

So what does the Bible say about miracles? Well, there are a LOT of miracles listed in the Bible! There are too many to list here, so read in the Bible from Genesis to Revelation if you want to catch them all. But I'll give some highlights here.

Creation (**Genesis 1-2**): God created everything from nothing! That's definitely not "explicable by natural or scientific laws." For more on that, check out Steve Risner's Worldview Warriors blog posts.

Isaac being born to Abraham and Sarah (**Genesis 21:1-7**): I don't know of any other 90- and 100-year-olds who have given birth, do you? This miracle occurred to fulfill God's promise to make Abraham's descendants into a great nation.

The parting of the Red Sea (**Exodus 14**): The people of Israel were trapped against the sea and the Egyptians were pursuing them, until God literally parted the waters so they could walk across on dry land. This wasn't like just crossing a little stream; it was approximately 9 miles they had to walk, through where the water should have been. This definitely defies the laws of nature, but for the good of God's people.

Jesus' conception and birth (**Luke 1:26-38**): With the advances of science today, a baby can be "conceived" in a test tube, but there still has to be material from a mother and a father present. In the conception of Jesus, there was no human father, but God Himself. This can't be explained by science.

The miracles that Jesus performed are numerous, including the healings I wrote about in the previous section. He also turned water into wine (**John 2:1-11**), walked on water (**Matthew 14:22-33**), fed 5,000 people from a small amount of food (**John 6:1-15**), and even raised Lazarus from the dead (**John 11:38-44**), just to name a few.

God is a miraculous God, and the Bible gives plenty of proof of that. He often does things that don't make sense in the natural world, so that we can see what a great God He is and how worthy He is of our praise. The God of the Bible is the same God we serve today, as He does not change, so does He still perform miracles today? I fully believe that He does, simply from healings I have witnessed to some people around me. God enjoys showing off His power so that His people will praise Him more.

What miracles have you seen God do in your life? What miracles are you hoping for God to do? What miracles are you praising God for?

What the Bible Says About
How to Treat Creation

Creation: it's all around us, and in fact literally is us! We know that God created everything (**Genesis 1-2**) - humans, nature, the sun and moon, the stars. So when He gave us His Word in the Bible, what did He tell us about how we should treat this amazing creation?

Genesis 2:15 says, "The Lord God took the man and put him in the Garden of Eden to work it and take care of it." The Hebrew word that's translated there as "work" can also mean labor or serve. The general idea of it is to work or serve with respect. The word that's translated there as "take care of" also means to guard or keep watch over. So in that statement, God is showing the man (Adam) and the rest of us that we should treat His creation with respect.

Numbers 35 talks about cities of refuge for the people of Israel where they can be safe, and **verses 33-34** say, "Do not pollute the land where you are. Bloodshed pollutes the land, and atonement cannot be made for the land on which blood has been shed, except by the blood of the one who shed it. Do not defile the land where you live and where I dwell, for I, the Lord, dwell among the Israelites." While that command was specific to the Israelites in that situation, we can take from it the idea that we should treat the land with respect. The Lord does dwell with us, and we should treat His creation well for that reason.

We know from **Psalm 24:1-2** that "The earth is the Lord's, and everything in it, the world, and all who live in it; for he founded it on the seas and established it on the waters." If someone gives you a gift, especially a person you greatly respect or admire, you would generally treat that gift with the utmost respect. How much more should we take care of this earth that God has given us! It is a gift to us, along with our very lives, from the almighty creator of the universe!

In **Exodus 23:10-11**, God gave Israel specific instructions regarding the farming of their land: "For six years you are to sow your fields and harvest the crops, but during the seventh year let the land lie unplowed and unused. Then the poor among your people may get food from it, and the wild animals may eat what is left. Do the same with your vineyard and your olive grove."

Deuteronomy 11:12 is talking about the promised land as the Israelites are about to cross into it. It says, "It is a land the Lord your God cares for; the eyes of the Lord your God are continually on it from the beginning of the year to its end." Again, that passage was written to that group of people specifically at that time, but the idea behind it is that God does care for the land, so we should treat it with respect.

God created this world for us as humans to inhabit, so simply because of that fact we should take care of it. It brings God glory when we take care of His creation. How are you glorifying God in your life by taking care of creation?

What the Bible Says About
How to Treat Animals

In the previous section, I wrote on what the Bible says about how to treat creation. In that post I mostly focused on the earth, but this week we're going to take a look at a specific part of that: what the Bible says about how to treat animals.

Personally, I enjoy animals! Our household has 5 cats, 4 frogs, 2 bearded dragons, and 1 betta fish. I enjoy having all of them around, as they often provide a lot of entertainment for us.

There are many categories of animals in this world - household pets, working animals, and wild animals, just to name a few. Obviously, I will care for my household pets in a different way than I would treat animals in the wild. But what does the Bible say about how we should treat animals?

Proverbs 12:10 says, "The righteous care for the needs of their animals, but the kindest acts of the wicked are cruel." The book of Proverbs often uses the contrast of "the righteous" versus "the wicked" to show the reader what they should do versus what they should not do. We should care for the needs of animals that are entrusted to our care.

But we also know from **Genesis 1:26-28** that mankind was created to have dominion over the animals, so they should not be given equal value to humans.

Animals were equivalent to livelihood back in the Old Testament, so they were often treated as prized possessions. With animals, you could be provided with meat, milk, and extra muscle to plow your fields. God shared animal care lessons with the people in **Exodus 23:5** ("If you see the donkey of someone who hates you fallen down under its load, do not leave it there; be sure you help them with it"), **Proverbs 27:23** ("Be sure you know the condition of your flocks, give careful attention to your herds"), **Deuteronomy 25:4** ("Do not muzzle an ox while it is treading out the grain"), and **Exodus 23:12** ("Six days do your work, but on the seventh day do not work, so that your ox and your donkey may rest, and so that the slave born in your household and the foreigner living among you may be refreshed") just to name a few.

We also see in both **Deuteronomy 27:21** and **Leviticus 18:23** that beastiality (having sexual relations with an animal) is a sin to God and also cruel to animals.

There are a few "famous" stories in the Bible in which animals play a significant role as well. Of course there's Noah's ark (**Genesis 6-9**), where two of every land-dwelling animal went with Noah and his family onto the ark to be saved from the flood. The story of Balaam and his donkey is an entertaining one that I'd encourage you to go read in **Numbers 22:21-41**. The story of Jonah just wouldn't be the same without the big fish in **Jonah 1:17**. The story of Jesus' triumphal entry (**Matthew 21:1-11**) into Jerusalem before He was crucified later that week would have different meaning without Jesus riding on a colt.

Animals are part of God's creation, and God cares for them, too: "Are not two sparrows sold for a penny? Yet not one of them will fall to the ground outside your Father's care" (**Matthew 10:29**). When we treat animals with love and respect, we are treating our creator God with love and respect. We don't have to all be animal lovers and have a zoo full of pets in our homes, but we can definitely treat all the animals we encounter with respect.

What the Bible Says About
Eating Animals

In the previous section, I wrote on what the Bible says about how to treat animals. We know that God created the animals, and He cares for them. But what about when it comes to eating animals - killing them for our food? What does the Bible say about that?

In **Genesis 1:28**, right after God created humans, "God blessed them and said to them, 'Be fruitful and increase in number; fill the earth and subdue it. Rule over the fish in the sea and the birds in the sky and over every living creature that moves on the ground.'" Humans are the pinnacle of God's creation, and we were created to rule over the animals. We were not created to treat them as equals, but to have dominion over them. Having dominion does not mean ruling like a dictator and exploiting something, but having a proper responsibility over them.

Before sin entered the world, there was no death, so animals would not have been killed in order to be eaten. But after Adam and Eve sinned, that all changed. The first death was an animal that was killed so its skin could make their clothing, now that it mattered that they weren't wearing any.

A bit later, right after the great flood, **Genesis 9:1-4** records this: "Then God blessed Noah and his sons, saying to them, 'Be fruitful and increase in number and fill the earth. The fear and dread of you will fall on all the beasts of the earth, and on all the birds in the sky, on every creature that moves along the ground, and on all the fish in the sea; they are given into your hands. Everything that lives and moves about will be food for you. Just as I gave you the green plants, I now give you everything. But you must not eat meat that has its lifeblood still in it.'" This makes it clear that it's now just fine for humans to eat animals.

In the **Leviticus 11**, God gives Israel a list of the clean and unclean animals, explaining which they are allowed to eat and which they are not allowed to eat. In that time and culture, things were very different than they are now regarding food. For one, they didn't have refrigeration to properly preserve meats that would easily spoil in the Middle Eastern heat. They also didn't have as thorough of cooking methods or a way to check proper meat temperatures as we do today. So, one reason God gave them these rules was to help them survive and not get sick from what they ate. This was also a way for the Israelites to show their devotion to God through their actions, since they were living under the Law and before the sacrifice of Jesus.

But what about now? In **Acts 10**, the apostle Peter had a vision where God showed him that animals are no longer either clean or unclean; that distinction is no longer necessary, just as the distinction between Jew and Gentile was no longer necessary. Because of Jesus' sacrificial death and resurrection, all people could be saved! These specific rules given to the Israelites about unclean animals no longer apply to us today, in our time and culture.

What about Jesus? Would he have eaten animals? While the Scriptures don't give us a detailed diet that Jesus ate, we do know that He ate fish after His resurrection, as recorded in **Luke 24:42-43** and **John 21**. Jesus likely would not have helped the disciples catch so many fish if he didn't believe they should be eaten.

In **1 Corinthians 8**, Paul writes to the church at Corinth about eating meat from sacrifices that were made to idols. He concludes that it's perfectly fine, as long as it does not cause you or those around you to stumble in the faith.

So the Bible clearly tells us that it's fine to eat meat. But what about those who choose to be vegetarian or even vegan? **Romans 14:2-3** says, "One person's faith allows them to eat anything, but another, whose faith is weak, eats only vegetables. The one who eats everything must not treat with contempt the one who does not, and the one who does not eat everything must not judge the one who does, for God has accepted them." This doesn't mean that vegetarians have weak faith; this means that we should not judge others critically for their dietary choices. We know that we are to treat animals well, and some live that out in their lives by choosing not to eat them.

Whatever our preference on eating meat, we should always be seeking to glorify God and strengthen our faith and the faith of others in all areas of life, whether we do so while eating a cheeseburger or a salad. "So whether you eat or drink or whatever you do, do it all for the glory of God" (**1 Corinthians 10:31**).

What the Bible Says About
Rainbows

Rainbows were one of my favorite things to draw as a kid, and I've always loved all the colors (as long as the colors are in the right order, of course). When I was growing up, rainbows were always considered a beautiful thing and a reminder of God's promises, but that has changed somewhat today with the LGBTQ movement adopting the rainbow as their symbol.

As a follower of Jesus Christ, it is important to base our beliefs on what the Bible says rather than what culture says. So, what does the Bible say about rainbows?

By far the most prominent rainbow reference in the Bible is right after the story of Noah's ark and the big flood found in **Genesis 6-9**. Specifically, **Genesis 9:12-16** says, "And God said, "This is the sign of the covenant I am making between me and you and every living creature with you, a covenant for all generations to come: I have set my rainbow in the clouds, and it will be the sign of the covenant between me and the earth. Whenever I bring clouds over the earth and the rainbow appears in the clouds, I will remember my covenant between me and you and all living creatures of every kind. Never again will the waters become a flood to destroy all life. Whenever the rainbow appears in the clouds, I will see it and remember the everlasting covenant between God and all living creatures of every kind on the earth."

Scientifically, today we know that rainbows appear in the sky because of reflection and refraction of sunlight when it hits water droplets, such as when the sun first comes out and there's still a bit of rain coming down. But we can also look at that rainbow as a remembrance of the promise that God made to Noah many generations ago: that He will never again destroy all life on earth with a flood. We know that God is faithful to His Word, and while there have been localized floods that do much damage (including in Findlay, Ohio, where I live), there has never again been a flood that destroyed nearly the whole planet like the one recorded in Genesis.

The next mention of a rainbow in the Bible is in the prophet Ezekiel's first vision. **Ezekiel 1:25-28** says, "Then there came a voice from above the vault over their heads as they stood with lowered wings. Above the vault over their heads was what looked like a throne of lapis lazuli, and high above on the throne was a figure like that of a man. I saw that from what appeared to be his waist up he looked like glowing metal, as if full of fire, and that from there down he looked like fire; and brilliant light surrounded him. Like the appearance of a rainbow in the clouds on a rainy day, so was the radiance around him." Here, the rainbow is a descriptive term to show the brilliance and radiance that surrounds this figure in his vision.

The final mentions of a rainbow in the Bible are in the book of Revelation. **Revelation 4:3**, referring to the scene John saw in the throne room of heaven, says, "And the one who sat there [on the throne] had the appearance of jasper and ruby. A rainbow that shone like an emerald encircled the throne." Later, **Revelation 10:1** tells us, "Then I saw another mighty angel coming down from heaven. He was robed in a cloud, with a rainbow above his head; his face was like the sun, and his legs were like fiery pillars." In these instances, the rainbow is seen again as a symbol of hope and of God's love, glory, and majesty.

What does the rainbow mean in your life? Does your interpretation of that refer to God's faithfulness and His glory and majesty, or something else? I encourage you to take a look deeper at what the Bible says, even when it may be counter-cultural.

What the Bible Says About
Different Languages

I love languages. I didn't always realize I loved them, but apparently I did. When I was in 7th grade, I made up my own language, both an alphabet and a spoken language (though I was really the only one who spoke it, since no one else wanted to really learn it). In high school, I excelled in Spanish class and even took a year beyond what was required. I took more Spanish classes in college and pondered a minor in the language, but then decided against it so I could focus more on my engineering classes. A few years later, when I was headed to seminary, I was afraid of Greek since a relative of mine struggled with it a few years prior to that. But by the end of the term, I was still waiting for it to get difficult! That was when it finally occurred to me that God had given me a gift for languages, and since then I have immensely enjoyed learning and teaching Biblical Hebrew as well.

Not everyone enjoys languages like I do, but what does the Bible say about them? To start, we should look at where different languages came from, which can be found in **Genesis 11:1-9**. That is the story of the Tower of Babel, which starts by telling us that "the whole world had one language and a common speech" (**verse 1**). Just when humanity had a good thing going with just one language, they had to go and mess it up. They got together and tried to build a tower that would reach God. To keep them from succeeding, God confused their languages and scattered them to different places.

The cool thing is how God tends to bring things full circle. A few centuries later, Jesus had come to earth, lived His life, died, was raised again, then ascended to heaven. Shortly after that, the disciples received the Holy Spirit on the day of Pentecost and began to speak to a large crowd, full of people who spoke a variety of different languages. Every person in the crowd was able to understand them! The same God who confused the languages back in **Genesis 11** also un-confused the languages in **Acts 2** to share the gospel message of Jesus with thousands of people all at one time.

Another story that has to do with language in the Bible is in **Judges 12:1-7**. In that story, a simple pronunciation difference determined which side you were on in a civil war among Israel.

Of course, the whole Bible is made up of language as well. The Bible is God's Word given to us in written form, and anything written has to be in a language. The Old Testament was originally written mostly in the ancient Hebrew language with some Aramaic, while the New Testament was originally written in Koine Greek. Today, the Bible has been fully translated into over 670 languages (and the New Testament into over 1500 languages), thanks to the work of many people and organizations, but it is still God's Word.

I would encourage everyone to learn it in its original languages as there is so much depth and richness there, but if that's not a skill you have, then praise God for those who do enjoy languages and have provided you with multiple English translations for you to read and to bring you closer to God!

What the Bible Says About
Entertainment

The entertainment industry is big business in today's world. In 2017, we Americans spent $11 billion at the box office, the recorded music industry was worth over $18 billion, video game revenue was over $23 billion, and book sales were over $37 billion. If you add up all those numbers, the entertainment industry as a whole was worth over $89 billion dollars last year - I'd say that's definitely big business!

However, "entertainment" is a relatively new thing. Until this modern area, people spent much of their time working, and when they weren't working they were likely taking care of things related to their survival. Free time and entertainment weren't part of daily lives until the 20th century when we developed technology that made working for survival easier. It was not until advances in technology in the 20th century that we had the capability to have recorded music, then movies, then video games. So, because of all this, the Bible does not speak directly to entertainment, since it didn't really exist in Biblical times like it does now.

But even if the Bible doesn't speak directly to entertainment, it does give us some guidelines to follow as we have the opportunity to entertain ourselves.

First of all, **Colossians 3:17** should be our guiding principle: "And whatever you do, whether in word or deed, do it all in the name of the Lord Jesus, giving thanks to God the Father through him." When we entertain ourselves, are you doing it all in the name of Jesus and giving thanks to God through the choices you make?

Along with that, **Philippians 4:8** says, "Finally, brothers and sisters, whatever is true, whatever is noble, whatever is right, whatever is pure, whatever is lovely, whatever is admirable — if anything is excellent or praiseworthy — think about such things." Think about the last movie you saw or video game you played; was it true, noble, right, pure, lovely, or admirable? Even if it's just a few hours of entertainment, your brain was focused on it during that time. We are commanded to think on that which is right and holy.

Not only that, but our entertainment choices can affect others as well. In **1 Corinthians 8**, Paul writes to the church at Corinth about eating food sacrificed to idols, which was a big issue for them. **Verse 9** says, "Be careful, however, that the exercise of your rights does not become a stumbling block to the weak." The principle we can take from this is that the freedom we have to relax and be entertained in our free time should not cause others to stumble in their walk. You may be a mature enough Christian that you can listen to certain music and remain strong in your faith, but someone around you may be weaker and your choices could cause them to stumble.

Matthew 6:24 says, "No one can serve two masters. Either you will hate the one and love the other, or you will be devoted to the one and despise the other. You cannot serve both God and money." We must be careful that our entertainment does not become our master, since we cannot serve entertainment and serve God at the same time. We must be careful that we do not put our own entertainment as a higher priority in life than God is.

Does that mean we should never watch movies, play video games, or listen to music? Well, the answer really depends on the message of those things and the attitude of our hearts. **Ephesians 5:8-11** tells us, "For you were once darkness, but now you are light in the Lord. Live as children of light (for the fruit of the light consists in all goodness, righteousness and truth) and find out what pleases the Lord. Have nothing to do with the fruitless deeds of darkness, but rather expose them." If the entertainment we choose is part of the "fruitless deeds of darkness," then we shouldn't bring those things into our lives. We are walking in the light of the Lord, and we should live as such.

Entertainment in and of itself is not evil. If our attitude is right and we are still honoring God with the entertainment choices we make, then we can enjoy its part in our lives. But as we've seen, the Bible clearly warns against letting our life choices (whether entertainment or otherwise) draw us away from Him. What kind of choices are you making for your entertainment?

What the Bible Says About
Satan

While God created the world to be good and perfect, we know that evil exists in this world. The main adversary against God is Satan, also known as the devil, Lucifer, and some other names. Since good versus evil is one of the main themes of the Bible, Satan is talked about a fair amount.

The first time we see Satan in the Bible is in **Genesis 3** in the Garden of Eden, when he comes to tempt Adam and Eve. He shows up in the form of a serpent and lies to the first humans that they could be like God by eating the fruit God told them not to eat. This leads many scholars to believe that Satan was already fallen and banished from heaven even before the creation of the world, though we don't have Biblical evidence to prove that.

We see Satan again in the beginning of the story of **Job**. Satan believes that he can get Job to curse God by afflicting him with all sorts of maladies, and God says that Job will remain faithful. (Spoiler alert: God won that bet.) The Hebrew word for Satan in this passage means "the adversary," the one who is against God.

In the New Testament, we see Satan described as "the prince of this world" (**John 14:30**), "the god of this age" (**2 Corinthians 4:4**), and "the ruler of the kingdom of the air" (**Ephesians 2:2**).

In both **Matthew 4:1-11** and **Luke 4:1-13**, we see accounts of Satan tempting Jesus in the wilderness. Satan tries to get Jesus to sin multiple times, so that Jesus would mess up and not be the perfect sacrifice for our sins according to God's plan. (Spoiler alert: Jesus won that battle.)

Satan was the root cause of Judas Iscariot betraying Jesus before His crucifixion, as we read in **Luke 22:1-6**. But what Satan determined to use for evil, God used for good, to complete His plan for our salvation. Jesus had to die in order to be raised again for us to have eternal life, and Judas and Satan played roles in that.

Jesus came for the purpose of destroying Satan's works. **1 John 3:8** says, "The one who does what is sinful is of the devil, because the devil has been sinning from the beginning. The reason the Son of God appeared was to destroy the devil's work." **John 10:10** says, "The thief [Satan] comes only to steal and kill and destroy; I [Jesus] have come that they may have life, and have it to the full."

But Satan wasn't just present in Biblical times; he is still active in our world today, trying to lure believers away from God. **1 Peter 5:8-9** says, "Be alert and of sober mind. Your enemy the devil prowls around like a roaring lion looking for someone to devour. Resist him, standing firm in the faith, because you know that the family of believers throughout the world is undergoing the same kind of sufferings." Everyone who believes in Jesus is being tempted by Satan, even today, but we have the power of Christ to be able to resist his temptations.

Ultimately, what will happen to Satan? He will be destroyed and thrown into the burning lake of sulfur. You can read about Satan's ultimate demise in **Revelation 20:1-10**. But until the end of the world, Satan will still be a part of it, tempting us each and every day. Until then, "Submit yourselves, then, to God. Resist the devil, and he will flee from you" (**James 4:7**).

What the Bible Says About
Addictions

Addictions are a prominent topic in today's world. When you hear the word "addiction," you probably immediately think of drug addiction, smoking, alcohol addiction, or things like that. But there are many other addictions that could grab ahold of our lives. We could be addicted to our phones, junk food, attention from other people, or all sorts of things. Addiction is part of our sinful human nature, and it is very much a fleshly desire.

The Bible does not address addiction specifically, but it does address temptation, and addiction is one form of temptation. We know that sin and evil come from the devil (**1 John 2:16**), but we have the power to resist temptation through the submission of our lives to God (**James 4:7**).

Galatians 5:16 says, "So I say, walk by the Spirit, and you will not gratify the desires of the flesh." If we're truly and fully walking in the ways of God's Spirit, we won't have the desire to gratify what the flesh wants. But while we live in this world, our natural tendency is to fulfill our own desires. It takes a stronger faith and trust in God to turn away from that kind of temptation.

Ephesians 5:18 tells us, "Do not get drunk on wine, which leads to debauchery. Instead, be filled with the Spirit." We can make choices in life whether to put ourselves into a potentially addictive situation or not. We can choose the addiction, or instead we can choose to be filled with God's Spirit.

Romans 6:6-7 says, "For we know that our old self was crucified with him so that the body ruled by sin might be done away with, that we should no longer be slaves to sin—because anyone who has died has been set free from sin." We are set free from our sin in

Christ and we are no longer slaves to it. Through Christ, we have the power to break any addiction we have in our lives.

1 Corinthians 10:13 says, "No temptation has overtaken you except what is common to mankind. And God is faithful; he will not let you be tempted beyond what you can bear. But when you are tempted, he will also provide a way out so that you can endure it." We know we will be tempted, because that is part of living in this world. But with God, we will have a way to get out of that temptation if we make the right choice.

Psalm 50:15 encourages us to, "Call on me [God] in the day of trouble; I will deliver you, and you will honor me." We know that God will ultimately deliver us when we call on Him and desire to live our lives to give Him honor and glory.

Are you sensing a theme yet? We will have sin and addictions in this world, but God is bigger and more powerful than them. We could very easily let this get us down, knowing that while we're in this world we'll have to constantly face temptations and potentially addictions. But instead, we should have a different attitude:

"Not only so, but we also glory in our sufferings, because we know that suffering produces perseverance; perseverance, character; and character, hope. And hope does not put us to shame, because God's love has been poured out into our hearts through the Holy Spirit, who has been given to us" (**Romans 5:3-5**).

"Consider it pure joy, my brothers and sisters, whenever you face trials of many kinds, because you know that the testing of your faith produces perseverance. Let perseverance finish its work so that you may be mature and complete, not lacking anything" (**James 1:2-4**).

But, all this is generally easier said than done. As Jesus told His disciples while they were waiting for Him as He prayed in the Garden of Gethsemane before His crucifixion, "Watch and pray so that you will not fall into temptation. The spirit is willing, but the flesh is weak." (**Matthew 26:41**). We need to be on guard for any kind of temptation, especially addictions: "Be alert and of sober mind. Your enemy the devil prowls around like a roaring lion looking for someone to devour" (**1 Peter 5:8**).

Take a look at your life and see what addictions you may be struggling with. Pray to God and work on deepening your relationship with Him, so that you will have His power to fight those addictions.

What the Bible Says About
Gender

Our culture keeps trying to redefine gender roles, so I hope this writing will help you maintain a Biblical foundation regarding gender.

Any Biblical discussion on gender has to start back at the beginning, at Creation. **Genesis 1:26-27** says, "Then God said, 'Let us make mankind in our image, in our likeness, so that they may rule over the fish in the sea and the birds in the sky, over the livestock and all the wild animals, and over all the creatures that move along the ground.' So God created mankind in his own image, in the image of God he created them; male and female he created them." God created humankind in His image, and He created us with two genders: male and female. This creation was "very good" (**Genesis 1:31**).

While the Bible does support science as we know it today, the purpose of the Bible is not to be a biology textbook so it does not provide anatomical details as to what defines a male or a female. But it is very clear that humankind was created with those two genders.

There are many passages in the Bible that give instructions based on gender roles, such as instructions to husbands and wives. One passage with such instructions is **Ephesians 5:25-33**. That passage discusses both the human relationship of husbands and wives and the spiritual relationship of Jesus Christ and the Church.

Some believe that the Bible considers men to be more important than women. It is true that the Bible was written to a patriarchal (male-dominated) society, but does that mean God favors males over females? I wrote a blog post on that a couple years ago, so for more on that aspect of gender, you can go to the Worldview Warrior blog and read my post titled "Why Does God Hate Women?".

But when it comes to having a saving faith in Jesus Christ, a person's gender doesn't matter. **Galatians 3:26-29** says, "So in Christ Jesus you are all children of God through faith, for all of you who were baptized into Christ have clothed yourselves with Christ. There is neither Jew nor Gentile, neither slave nor free, nor is there male and female, for you are all one in Christ Jesus. If you belong to Christ, then you are Abraham's seed, and heirs according to the promise."

As believers in Christ, we are all called to "Follow God's example, therefore, as dearly loved children and walk in the way of love, just as Christ loved us and gave himself up for us as a fragrant offering and sacrifice to God" (**Ephesians 5:1-2**). That's what the life of a follower of Christ should be all about.

Are you living your life as an example of the love of Christ to all people, regardless of their gender? If you are a follower of Jesus, what are you doing to support the Biblical worldview in gender discussions happening in our culture today?

What the Bible Says About
Peace

"Shalom!" This is the traditional Jewish greeting, which can be used as a "hello" or a "goodbye," but literally the word "shalom" is Hebrew for "peace." I think it's a great sentiment to wish peace to someone when you greet them, whether coming or going. But what does the Bible say about peace? What kind of peace are we talking about?

The word "peace" occurs hundreds of times in the Bible, so I will not list all of them in this chapter. There are different kinds of peace discussed as well.

One type of peace spoken of in the Bible is regarding relationships. There can be peace between people, such as in **Genesis 34:21** where Jacob's sons make a deal with the Hivites to live peacefully together. Peace can also happen between nations, such as in **1 Kings 5:12** where Solomon and the nation of Israel has a peaceful agreement with Hiram, who supplied logs for the construction of the temple. We also see God promising peace to His people, such as in **Psalm 85:8**: "I will listen to what God the Lord says; he promises peace to his people, his faithful servants—but let them not turn to folly."

Ultimately, true peace only comes from God. **Psalm 4:8** says, "In peace I will lie down and sleep, for you alone, Lord, make me dwell in safety." **2 Thessalonians 3:16** says, "Now may the Lord of peace himself give you peace at all times and in every way. The Lord be with all of you." **Romans 15:13** says, "May the God of hope fill you with all joy and peace as you trust in him, so that you may overflow with hope by the power of the Holy Spirit."

Jesus was foretold to be the Prince of Peace (**Isaiah 9:6**), and at His birth the angels proclaimed peace on Earth (**Luke 2:14**). In **John 14:27** Jesus said, "Peace I leave with you; my peace I give you. I do not give to you as the world gives. Do not let your hearts be troubled and do not be afraid." A bit later in the same discourse (**John 16:33**) Jesus said, "I have told you these things, so that in me you may have peace. In this world you will have trouble. But take heart! I have overcome the world."

We are commanded to live in peace as much as we can. **Romans 14:19** says, "Let us therefore make every effort to do what leads to peace and to mutual edification." We are also told to, "Let the peace of Christ rule in your hearts, since as members of one body you were called to peace. And be thankful" (**Colossians 3:15**). Peace should be a way of life for those who follow Jesus Christ, as He is the embodiment of peace.

Because of sin in the world, there will continue to be conflicts and a lack of peace until Jesus comes back again to instill lasting peace as in **Isaiah 11:1-10**. Jesus came to earth to take on our punishment and die so that there may be peace (**Isaiah 53:3**).

Are you living a life governed by peace of Jesus, or by the flesh? **Romans 8:6** says, "The mind governed by the flesh is death, but the mind governed by the Spirit is life and peace." I encourage you to pursue Jesus' peace in your life this week. "And the peace of God, which transcends all understanding, will guard your hearts and your minds in Christ Jesus" (**Philippians 4:7**).

What the Bible Says About
Faith

We've written a lot about the topic of faith here at Worldview Warriors. I've written about how a person has faith, living out our faith in the public square, who our faith is in, and many of my blog posts on the book of Romans from 2015 dealt with faith. Fellow writer Logan Ames has written a book called *Heroes of the Faith* based on **Hebrews 11**.

Faith is a pretty important aspect of being a follower of Jesus, so naturally the Bible has a lot to say about it. To start, let's see how the Bible defines faith: "Now faith is confidence in what we hope for and assurance about what we do not see" (**Hebrews 11:1**). A few verses later in **Hebrews 11:6** we see that, "And without faith it is impossible to please God, because anyone who comes to him must believe that he exists and that he rewards those who earnestly seek him." We cannot be a believer in God without faith, because we have to believe that He exists before we can follow Him.

Faith is essential for salvation. In **Ephesians 2:8-9**, Paul writes that, "For it is by grace you have been saved, through faith — and this is not from yourselves, it is the gift of God — not by works, so that no one can boast." **1 Peter 1:8-9** says, "Though you have not seen him, you love him; and even though you do not see him now, you believe in him and are filled with an inexpressible and glorious joy, for you are receiving the end result of your faith, the salvation of your souls."

Where does faith come from? It comes from hearing the message of God. "If you declare with your mouth, 'Jesus is Lord,' and believe in your heart that God raised him from the dead, you will be saved. For it is with your heart that you believe and are justified, and it is with your mouth that you profess your faith and are saved. ...

Consequently, faith comes from hearing the message, and the message is heard through the word about Christ." (**Romans 10:9-10, 17**).

Jesus tells us that our faith has mighty power. "'Have faith in God,' Jesus answered. 'Truly I tell you, if anyone says to this mountain, 'Go, throw yourself into the sea,' and does not doubt in their heart but believes that what they say will happen, it will be done for them. Therefore I tell you, whatever you ask for in prayer, believe that you have received it, and it will be yours'" (**Mark 11:22-24**). In **Luke 7:1-10**, we see that the centurion's faith is what caused Jesus to heal his servant. In **Matthew 21:18-22**, Jesus instructs His disciples that they can do amazing things when they truly have faith.

How are we to live out our faith? **James 2:14-26** tells us that our faith is shown through our works. "As the body without the spirit is dead, so faith without deeds is dead" (**James 2:26**). We should live by our faith in God, who is unseen, rather than living by the things we see (**2 Corinthians 5:7**). While not using the actual word for faith, **Proverbs 3:5-6** still demonstrates living out our faith: "Trust in the Lord with all your heart and lean not on your own understanding; in all your ways submit to him, and he will make your paths straight."

These passages I've referenced are just some of the ones that explicitly deal with faith, but the entire Bible is filled with examples of people living out their faith, or not having faith in God and facing the consequences. I encourage you to strengthen your faith by learning about those in the Bible who have lived out their faith well.

What the Bible Says About
Mercy

What is mercy? It's a word we may have difficulty defining, but we always appreciate receiving mercy! Google's dictionary defines mercy as "compassion or forgiveness shown toward someone whom it is within one's power to punish or harm." Showing mercy means we could harm someone, but we choose not to. That does sound like a pretty Biblical and Christian concept, don't you think? So what does the Bible actually say about mercy?

Many of the times the Bible speaks of mercy it's in the New Testament, but it definitely shows up in the Old Testament, too. **Micah 6:8** tells us that God commands us to show mercy: "He has shown you, O mortal, what is good. And what does the Lord require of you? To act justly and to love mercy and to walk humbly with your God." We also see mercy in **Lamentations 3:22-23**: "Because of the Lord's great love we are not consumed, for his compassions [mercies] never fail. They are new every morning; great is your faithfulness."

David pleaded with God to show him mercy in **Psalm 40:11**: "Do not withhold your mercy from me, Lord; may your love and faithfulness always protect me." David also explains God's mercy in **Psalm 25:6-7**: "Remember, Lord, your great mercy and love, for they are from of old. Do not remember the sins of my youth and my rebellious ways; according to your love remember me, for you, Lord, are good."

Some translations of **Psalm 23:6** use the word "mercy," while others use "love." The word there in the Hebrew is *hesed*, which we really don't have a good English word for. The concept of *hesed* is a combination of mercy, love, and kindness. Wherever *hesed* is used, the translators have to decide which English word fits best, so sometimes we see mercy and other times they use other words.

While it doesn't use the specific word "mercy," one of the most famous Bible passages of **John 3:16-17** explains God's mercy toward us: "For God so loved the world that he gave his one and only Son, that whoever believes in him shall not perish but have eternal life. For God did not send his Son into the world to condemn the world, but to save the world through him."

Mercy is included as part of the Beatitudes in **Matthew 5**: "Blessed are the merciful for they will be shown mercy" (**Matthew 5:7**). When speaking about loving your enemies, Jesus commanded us to "Be merciful, just as your Father is merciful" (**Luke 6:36**). We are also instructed to be merciful to others if we want to be shown mercy, in **James 2:12-13**: "Speak and act as those who are going to be judged by the law that gives freedom, because judgment without mercy will be shown to anyone who has not been merciful. Mercy triumphs over judgment."

Even the single-chapter book of Jude talks about showing mercy in **Jude 1:22-23**: "Be merciful to those who doubt; save others by snatching them from the fire; to others show mercy, mixed with fear—hating even the clothing stained by corrupted flesh."

Mercy goes hand-in-hand with God's grace, which you'll see in the next section. The Bible is full of God's mercy, because without Him being a merciful God, we humans would be too sinful to have a relationship with Him. I'll leave you with mercy as part of our salvation through Jesus, in **Ephesians 2:4-5**: "But because of his great love for us, God, who is rich in mercy, made us alive with Christ even when we were dead in transgressions—it is by grace you have been saved."

What the Bible Says About
Grace

This is one of those sections where I simply want to write: "What does the Bible say about grace? See: entire Bible." The entire Bible is full of the overarching story of God's grace toward humanity, told through the stories of individuals or nations and through the life of Jesus Himself. But in this writing, I'll try and highlight a few passages that speak specifically to God's grace and what it is.

One of my first few blog posts for Worldview Warriors back in 2011 was titled "Grace," and we as a ministry have written numerous other posts on that same topic. We touch on God's grace in many of our writings since it's such a primary focus of our Christian faith.

So what is grace? Simply put, it's undeserved favor. We have sinned and don't deserve to even be in relationship with God, much less be saved by Him, so it's only through His grace that we can receive that salvation. This is closely related with God's mercy, which I wrote about in the last section.

Ephesians 2:8-9 is one of the primary passages that explains salvation through God's grace: "For it is by grace you have been saved, through faith—and this is not from yourselves, it is the gift of God—not by works, so that no one can boast." (I'd encourage you to read the whole chapter of **Ephesians 2** to get an even better picture of God's grace.) Similarly, **Romans 11:6** says, "And if by grace, then it cannot be based on works; if it were, grace would no longer be grace." Grace means we do nothing to earn it; it's not based at all on our works.

Titus 2:11-14 speaks of the effects of God's grace in our lives: "For the grace of God has appeared that offers salvation to all people. It teaches us to say 'No' to ungodliness and worldly passions, and to live self-controlled, upright and godly lives in this present age, while we wait for the blessed hope — the appearing of the glory of our great God and Savior, Jesus Christ, who gave himself for us to redeem us from all wickedness and to purify for himself a people that are his very own, eager to do what is good."

Receiving God's grace should not cause us to sin more because we know we'll receive it. **Romans 6:1-2** says, "What shall we say, then? Shall we go on sinning so that grace may increase? By no means! We are those who have died to sin; how can we live in it any longer?"

In his second letter to Timothy, Paul writes, "So do not be ashamed of the testimony about our Lord or of me his prisoner. Rather, join with me in suffering for the gospel, by the power of God. He has saved us and called us to a holy life — not because of anything we have done but because of his own purpose and grace. This grace was given us in Christ Jesus before the beginning of time, but it has now been revealed through the appearing of our Savior, Christ Jesus, who has destroyed death and has brought life and immortality to light through the gospel" (**2 Timothy 1:8-10**).

I encourage you this week to live out God's grace in your life, the favor He gives you that you don't deserve at all.

What the Bible Says About
the Poor

As long as there is money in this world, there will be some people who have a lot of it and some who don't have much of it. Here, we're taking a look at what the Bible says about the poor.

Deuteronomy 15:11 tells us, "There will always be poor people in the land. Therefore I command you to be open handed toward your fellow Israelites who are poor and needy in your land." While that was obviously written directly to the people of Israel, the principles apply to us today as well. **1 John 3:17** says, "If anyone has material possessions and sees a brother or sister in need but has no pity on them, how can the love of God be in that person?"

In what's known as the parable of the sheep and goats in **Matthew 25:31-46**, Jesus shares that whenever we give to the poor, it's just like giving to Him. Similarly, **Proverbs 14:31** says, "Whoever oppresses the poor shows contempt for their Maker, but whoever is kind to the needy honors God." **Matthew 5:42** says, "Give to the one who asks you, and do not turn away from the one who wants to borrow from you."

How should we give to those in need? **Matthew 6:1-4** says, "Be careful not to practice your righteousness in front of others to be seen by them. If you do, you will have no reward from your Father in heaven. So when you give to the needy, do not announce it with trumpets, as the hypocrites do in the synagogues and on the streets, to be honored by others. Truly I tell you, they have received their reward in full. But when you give to the needy, do not let your left hand know what your right hand is doing, so that your giving may be in secret. Then your Father, who sees what is done in secret, will reward you."

In **Luke 6:38** Jesus says, "Give, and it will be given to you. A good measure, pressed down, shaken together and running over, will be poured into your lap. For with the measure you use, it will be measured to you." Toward the end of His earthly ministry, when Jesus' feet were anointed using a jar of expensive perfume and the disciples questioned the wastefulness, Jesus told them, "The poor you will always have with you, but you will not always have me." (**Matthew 26:11**).

The book of Proverbs has much wisdom on how we are to treat the poor. **Proverbs 22:22-23** says, "Do not exploit the poor because they are poor and do not crush the needy in court, for the Lord will take up their case and will exact life for life." **Proverbs 31:8-9** says, "Speak up for those who cannot speak for themselves, for the rights of all who are destitute. Speak up and judge fairly; defend the rights of the poor and needy." **Proverbs 19:17** says, "Whoever is kind to the poor lends to the Lord, and he will reward them for what they have done."

Jesus told His disciples, "Blessed are you who are poor, for yours is the kingdom of God. ... But woe to you who are rich, for you have already received your comfort" (**Luke 6:20, 24**). You don't have to be rich to inherit the Kingdom of God: "Listen, my dear brothers and sisters: Has not God chosen those who are poor in the eyes of the world to be rich in faith and to inherit the kingdom he promised those who love him?" (**James 2:5**). But we can still show our faith by helping those in need: "What good is it, my brothers and sisters, if someone claims to have faith but has no deeds? Can such faith save them? Suppose a brother or a sister is without clothes and daily food. If one of you says to them, "Go in peace; keep warm and well fed," but does nothing about their physical needs, what good is it? In the same way, faith by itself, if it is not accompanied by action, is dead" (**James 2:14-17**).

The key thing to remember when dealing with the poor is this: "A new command I give you: Love one another. As I have loved you, so you must love one another. By this everyone will know that you are my disciples, if you love one another" (**John 13:34-35**). First and foremost, we as followers of Jesus are called to be His disciples, which means showing God's love to others. Sometimes this may mean fulfilling their material needs, and other times this may mean helping them learn new skills to help themselves in life. The key is to be in relationship with Jesus so we know how to live out the love that He desires to show all people, whether rich or poor.

"For you know the grace of our Lord Jesus Christ, that though he was rich, yet for your sake he became poor, so that you through his poverty might become rich" (**2 Corinthians 8:9**).

What the Bible Says About
Conflict

Conflict: it happens to all of us, but none of us like it. Conflict exists because of sin in this world, so we'll have to deal with it our whole lives in various forms and with various people. So what does the Bible say about conflict?

"What causes fights and quarrels among you? Don't they come from your desires that battle within you? You desire but do not have, so you kill. You covet but you cannot get what you want, so you quarrel and fight. You do not have because you do not ask God" (**James 4:1-2**). That passage pretty much sums up why we have conflict; we look to others to fulfill our needs rather than looking to God, and we get frustrated when those needs are not fulfilled.

If we were all able to live perfect, sinless lives, conflict would not exist. "Get rid of all bitterness, rage and anger, brawling and slander, along with every form of malice. Be kind and compassionate to one another, forgiving each other, just as in Christ God forgave you" (**Ephesians 4:31-32**).

"Do nothing out of selfish ambition or vain conceit. Rather, in humility value others above yourselves, not looking to your own interests but each of you to the interests of the others" (**Philippians 2:3-4**).

"A new command I give you: Love one another. As I have loved you, so you must love one another" (**John 13:34**).

"My dear brothers and sisters, take note of this: Everyone should be quick to listen, slow to speak and slow to become angry, because human anger does not produce the righteousness that God desires" (**James 1:19-20**).

But, since we all mess up at that, we know we will have trouble and conflict in this world (**John 16:33**). So what can we do to resolve these conflicts?

One of the most common methods for dealing with conflict is described in detail in **Matthew 18:15-17**: "If your brother or sister sins, go and point out their fault, just between the two of you. If they listen to you, you have won them over. But if they will not listen, take one or two others along, so that 'every matter may be established by the testimony of two or three witnesses.' If they still refuse to listen, tell it to the church; and if they refuse to listen even to the church, treat them as you would a pagan or a tax collector."

The other key method for conflict resolution is forgiveness. "If your brother or sister sins against you, rebuke them; and if they repent, forgive them. Even if they sin against you seven times in a day and seven times come back to you saying 'I repent,' you must forgive them" (**Luke 17:3-4**).

Sometimes, it is best to simply overlook the wrong that someone has done to you. **Proverbs 19:11** says, "A person's wisdom yields patience; it is to one's glory to overlook an offense." But, we have to be careful that that overlooking doesn't take root and turn into bitterness that we will later have to overcome.

Sometimes we can avoid conflict simply by following these words of Jesus in **Matthew 5:38-42**: "You have heard that it was said, 'Eye for eye, and tooth for tooth.' But I tell you, do not resist an evil person. If anyone slaps you on the right cheek, turn to them the other cheek also. And if anyone wants to sue you and take your shirt, hand over your coat as well. If anyone forces you to go one mile, go with them two miles. Give to the one who asks you, and do not turn away from the one who wants to borrow from you."

Resolving conflict is so important that Jesus tells His followers to not even bring an offering to Him if we have unresolved conflict. "Therefore, if you are offering your gift at the altar and there remember that your brother or sister has something against you, leave your gift there in front of the altar. First go and be reconciled to them; then come and offer your gift" (**Matthew 5:23-24**).

How are you doing with conflict in your life? Are you causing it, avoiding it, or resolving it? As you go about your days, I encourage you to remember these words of the apostle Paul in **Colossians 3:12-13**: "Therefore, as God's chosen people, holy and dearly loved, clothe yourselves with compassion, kindness, humility, gentleness and patience. Bear with each other and forgive one another if any of you has a grievance against someone. Forgive as the Lord forgave you."

What the Bible Says About
Life and Death

If you're reading this post, then you definitely know something about life, because, well, you're alive. But we all have to deal with death in our lifetime, too - the death of friends, family members, and other loved ones, and ultimately facing our own death at some point. This can be hard to deal with, so as followers of Jesus we should be looking to Him and His Word for answers. So what does the Bible say about life and death?

First, let's start with life. We know that God created us and gave us life (**Genesis 2:4-25**). But because mankind messed up and turned away from God (**Genesis 3; Romans 5:12**), we all deserve death but can have life through faith in the work of Jesus (**Romans 6:23; John 3:16-17; John 14:6**). Because of this faith, we strive to live our lives as God wants us to, in obedience to Him (**Romans 12:2**).

But what about death? We will all die a physical death as our bodies wear out or some sort of trauma happens to cause it. But if we have faith in Jesus, then we don't need to fear the physical death, because then we will be able to live in close communion with God forever. However, if we don't have faith in Jesus, then we should be very afraid because we'll spend eternity completely separated from God. **Matthew 10:28** says, "Do not be afraid of those who kill the body but cannot kill the soul. Rather, be afraid of the One who can destroy both soul and body in hell."

In the story about the death of Lazarus (brother to Mary and Martha) in **John 11**, Jesus tells Martha, "I am the resurrection and the life. The one who believes in me will live, even though they die; and whoever lives by believing in me will never die" (**verses 25-26**). Lazarus died a physical death, Jesus raised him back to life, and however many years later, Lazarus still had to die another physical death. But if he had faith in Jesus as we believe he did, then he didn't have to fear the physical death because he would live forever with Jesus.

That's the good news - Jesus is Lord over both the living and the dead! **Romans 14:7-9** says, "For none of us lives for ourselves alone, and none of us dies for ourselves alone. If we live, we live for the Lord; and if we die, we die for the Lord. So, whether we live or die, we belong to the Lord. For this very reason, Christ died and returned to life so that he might be the Lord of both the dead and the living."

1 Corinthians 15:51-58 gives us confidence that Jesus has victory over death, and He shares that victory with us! This passages quotes **Hosea 13:14**, which says, "I will deliver this people from the power of the grave; I will redeem them from death. Where, O death, are your plagues? Where, O grave, is your destruction?"

How do we live in this victory over death? By living the life that Christ calls us to and living out our faith in Him. **Romans 8:13** says, "For if you live according to the flesh, you will die; but if by the Spirit you put to death the misdeeds of the body, you will live."

We see from his writings that the Apostle Paul wrestled with this concept of life and death a lot - likely because he was often imprisoned and the threat of physical death was an ever-present reality in his world. In **Philippians 1:21-24** he writes, "For to me, to live is Christ and to die is gain. If I am to go on living in the body, this will mean fruitful labor for me. Yet what shall I choose? I do not know! I am torn between the two: I desire to depart and be with Christ, which is better by far; but it is more necessary for you that I remain in the body."

When you are a follower of Jesus, death is not something to be feared. Be encouraged by more words on this from Paul in **2 Corinthians 5:6-9**: "Therefore we are always confident and know that as long as we are at home in the body we are away from the Lord. For we live by faith, not by sight. We are confident, I say, and would prefer to be away from the body and at home with the Lord. So we make it our goal to please him, whether we are at home in the body or away from it." Physical death is leaving this world, but it is also being united with Jesus forever!

To close, this truth from John in **1 John 5:12** pretty well sums it up: "Whoever has the Son has life; whoever does not have the Son of God does not have life." Be mindful of that as you go about however many days God has given you on this earth.

What the Bible Says About
Suicide

In the last section, I wrote about what the Bible says about life and death. Here, I want to address a different circumstance of that: suicide. This is a topic that we at Worldview Warriors have been asked about at various times and in various ways, so we want to address it for those of you struggling with this - whether pondering suicide yourself, or struggling with a loved one who committed suicide.

Some people seem to believe that suicide is an unforgivable sin, and because of it that person would definitely not go to heaven. What does the Bible say about that? Nothing that I can find. The determining factor of whether a person goes to heaven or to hell is their faith in Jesus, not the cause of their death. It can be argued that the act of committing suicide is done because one loses faith in Jesus, but again the Bible does not speak specifically to that. We know that God is the ultimate Judge and the one to decide the fate of every human being, and we have to trust that He is loving and just.

There are stories in the Bible of people committing suicide, or making someone kill them (which is basically the same thing). In **1 Samuel 31**, Saul fell on his own sword and killed himself, rather than face being captured by the Philistines. At the end of **Judges 9**, Abimelech makes his armor bearer kill him, rather than be killed due to injuries incurred by a woman. In **Judges 16**, Samson commits suicide (as well as the murder of thousands of Philistines) by literally bringing down the house. In **Matthew 27:1-5**, Judas Iscariot killed himself out of the guilt of betraying Jesus.

God isn't interested in finding technicalities to keep people out of heaven, like the method in which a person dies. He fully desires for everyone to join Him in heaven for all eternity (**1 Timothy 2:4; 2**

Peter 3:9). He loves and highly values EVERY person, including you! God desires to have relationship with us and has made each one of us for a good purpose (**Romans 8:28**).

In this world, there will be sin. There will be bad stuff that happens. There will be things that may make it difficult to see how you can go on with life. But, Jesus has overcome the world! He has promised to always be with us, through whatever struggles we may face.

Here are just some of promises God made to us to assure us of His presence with us:

Jesus tells us in **John 16:33**, "I have told you these things, so that in me you may have peace. In this world you will have trouble. But take heart! I have overcome the world."

We know that God will never leave us or forsake us (**Deuteronomy 31:6**).

Jesus will be with us always, even to the end of the age (**Matthew 28:18-20**).

Even though we walk through dark places, we don't need to fear because He is with us (**Psalm 23:4**).

Not even death can separate us from the love of God when we have faith in Him (**Romans 8:38-39**).

God is greater than anything we face in this world (**1 John 4:4**).

God will be with us, strengthen us, and help us, because He is our God (**Isaiah 41:10**).

God is near to us when even we're suffering, and He will deliver us (**Psalm 34:18-19**).

The best way to deal with the hopelessness that suicide stems from is to renew your hope in Jesus, the only one who is truly worth hoping in. If you are considering suicide, please get appropriate help through resources such as the National Suicide Prevention

Lifeline. Also, reach out to fellow believers to strengthen your relationship with Christ through their encouragement. Find a local Bible-believing church to encourage you and help you grow in your faith. If you don't have anyone close to you that you can reach out to regarding this, please contact us here at Worldview Warriors! Connect with us on Facebook or contact us through our website. We will help encourage you with God's truth about this or whatever struggle you may be having.

What the Bible Says About
Authority

Authority is one of those things that we all appreciate when it keeps things under control, but we also don't appreciate it when we feel as though it's oppressing us or keeping us from doing what we want to do. Authority comes in lots of forms such as teachers at school, your boss at work, those to protect us in law enforcement, and those who rule over us in local and national governments. But what does the Bible say about authority?

First and foremost, we know that all authority in heaven and on earth has been given to Jesus. Because of that, He gives us the authority and power (and the command) to go and make disciples of all nations (**Matthew 28:18-20**). "Therefore God exalted him to the highest place and gave him the name that is above every name, that at the name of Jesus every knee should bow, in heaven and on earth and under the earth, and every tongue acknowledge that Jesus Christ is Lord, to the glory of God the Father" (**Philippians 2:9-11**).

As for human authorities who govern over us, we see in **Romans 13:1-7** that Paul urges believers to obey the governing authorities. It's somewhat easy to submit to the authorities who govern over us when their rule lines up with God's Word. But what about when it doesn't?

1 Peter 2:13-18 says, "Submit yourselves for the Lord's sake to every human authority: whether to the emperor, as the supreme authority, or to governors, who are sent by him to punish those who do wrong and to commend those who do right. For it is God's will that by doing good you should silence the ignorant talk of foolish people. Live as free people, but do not use your freedom as a cover-up for evil; live as God's slaves. Show proper respect to everyone, love the family of believers, fear God, honor the emperor. Slaves, in reverent fear of God submit yourselves to your masters, not only to those who are good and considerate, but also to those who are harsh."

Ephesians 6:5-9 says, "Slaves, obey your earthly masters with respect and fear, and with sincerity of heart, just as you would obey Christ. Obey them not only to win their favor when their eye is on you, but as slaves of Christ, doing the will of God from your heart. Serve wholeheartedly, as if you were serving the Lord, not people, because you know that the Lord will reward each one for whatever good they do, whether they are slave or free. And masters, treat your slaves in the same way. Do not threaten them, since you know that he who is both their Master and yours is in heaven, and there is no favoritism with him."

While I would guess that most of the readers of this book are not in slavery, that was a more common situation in Biblical times so the Bible speaks on it a fair amount. But slavery back then was not the same as we think of slavery today. During Biblical times, slavery was generally only for a short time to pay off a debt, and then the slave was freed. Even though we're not technically enslaved, we can use the principles given in these passages when we are dealing with authorities such as bosses or teachers. Serve them as if we're serving God; do God's will by obeying them.

Paul gives us words of encouragement on dealing with authority in **1 Thessalonians 5:12-15**: "Now we ask you, brothers and sisters, to acknowledge those who work hard among you, who care for you in the Lord and who admonish you. Hold them in the highest regard in love because of their work. Live in peace with each other. And we urge you, brothers and sisters, warn those who are idle and disruptive, encourage the disheartened, help the weak, be patient with everyone. Make sure that nobody pays back wrong for wrong, but always strive to do what is good for each other and for everyone else."

The writer of Hebrews echoes this thought in **Hebrews 13:17**: "Have confidence in your leaders and submit to their authority, because they keep watch over you as those who must give an account. Do this so that their work will be a joy, not a burden, for that would be of no benefit to you." **Titus 3:1-2** also encourages us this way: "Remind the people to be subject to rulers and authorities, to be obedient, to be ready to do whatever is good, to slander no one, to be peaceable and considerate, and always to be gentle toward everyone."

In the book of Acts, Peter and the other apostles were often persecuted and thrown in jail for the sake of the Gospel. In one such instance, they are being questioned before the high priest and the Sanhedrin (some of their governing authorities) and they said, "We must obey God rather than human beings!" (**Acts 5:29**).

We see from Scripture that it's important to obey the human authorities that are over us, but when we have to choose between obeying God or mankind, we know that receiving God's reward in eternity is better than the temporary reward we'd receive for obeying humans and going against God. "Do not be afraid of those who kill the body but cannot kill the soul. Rather, be afraid of the One who can destroy both soul and body in hell" (**Matthew 10:28**).

What the Bible Says About
Free Will

Growing up in the church, we would often have events where there was a "free will" offering collected. Rather than charge a fee to attend the event, you could give whatever you wanted (if anything) toward the event's cost or for whatever cause funds were being raised. One of the pastors had a saying about free will offerings that I still remember (and sometimes use): "You got in free, so you will give an offering!"

So, what is "free will"? According to Google's dictionary, free will is defined as "the power of acting without the constraint of necessity or fate; the ability to act at one's own discretion." Free will is being autonomous and able to make our own decisions, not being controlled by some being in authority over us.

God created humans in His image (**Genesis 1:27**), so we all have the desire to choose good or evil, just as the first people Adam and Eve did. They knew the rules God had set for them (**Genesis 2:16-17**), and they broke those rules (**Genesis 3**). That was the first example of humans' free will being exercised.

Because of that original sin, our human nature generally chooses to go against God. The people of Israel continually had to make the choice to serve God or to serve their own selfish desires or the other peoples around them. **Deuteronomy 30:19-20** demonstrates this: "This day I call the heavens and the earth as witnesses against you that I have set before you life and death, blessings and curses. Now choose life, so that you and your children may live and that you may love the Lord your God, listen to his voice, and hold fast to him. For the Lord is your life, and he will give you many years in the land he swore to give to your fathers, Abraham, Isaac and Jacob."

Joshua 24:15 shows how Joshua and his household chose to serve God: "But if serving the Lord seems undesirable to you, then choose for yourselves this day whom you will serve, whether the gods your ancestors served beyond the Euphrates, or the gods of the Amorites, in whose land you are living. But as for me and my household, we will serve the Lord."

We, too, have the choice to repent from those evil actions and turn back to God (**Matthew 3:2; Matthew 4:17; Acts 3:19**). It is our choice to believe in Jesus and choose to follow Him, or to continually choose to turn away from Him (**1 John 3:23**). In **John 1:12-13** we see that we still have the option to be made right with God again: "Yet to all who did receive him, to those who believed in his name, he gave the right to become children of God — children born not of natural descent, nor of human decision or a husband's will, but born of God."

The apostle Paul struggled with his free will in **Romans 7:15-21**: "I do not understand what I do. For what I want to do I do not do, but what I hate I do. And if I do what I do not want to do, I agree that the law is good. As it is, it is no longer I myself who do it, but it is sin living in me. For I know that good itself does not dwell in me, that is, in my sinful nature. For I have the desire to do what is good, but I cannot carry it out. For I do not do the good I want to do, but the evil I do not want to do — this I keep on doing. Now if I do what I do not want to do, it is no longer I who do it, but it is sin living in me that does it. So I find this law at work: Although I want to do good, evil is right there with me." Just like each one of us, Paul had the choice to do what he knows is right or to go against that. He struggled with knowing what is right and desiring to do it, yet not being able to fully do that. That's the free will that God has given us.

Of course, we are not free to choose absolutely anything we want. I could choose to fly, but that doesn't give me the ability to do it. Our free will is still bound by the laws of nature and this world that God has created for us. We also need to be aware of God's natural law, where we will experience consequences for the choices that we're free to make. We will reap the consequences for our choices and actions in this world.

I often say, "Just because you can, doesn't mean you should." This pretty well sums up free will; we can make lots of choices that turn us away from God, but just because we CAN make those choices doesn't mean we SHOULD. Choose this day to love and serve God with your life!

What the Bible Says About
Truth

Truth is an important topic in our culture today. Many people say it's a subjective thing - what's true for you may not be true for me. I've written on the topic of absolute or relative truth on the Worldview Warriors blog, so I encourage you to find those posts if you want to read more on those topics. Here, we're going to focus on what the Bible says about truth.

Perhaps one of the most commonly known passages about truth is found in **John 8:32**: "Then you will know the truth, and the truth will set you free." If you look at the context of that passage, you'll see that Jesus spoke that line right after saying, "If you hold to my teaching, you are really my disciples" (**verse 31**). The truth comes from Jesus' teachings, and it will set us free when we are His disciples. Jesus and the Jews then have a discussion about sin and being Abraham's descendants, and Jesus ends His discourse with this: "Yet because I tell the truth, you do not believe me! Can any of you prove me guilty of sin? If I am telling the truth, why don't you believe me? Whoever belongs to God hears what God says. The reason you do not hear is that you do not belong to God" (**verses 45-47**). Jesus did not sin, so He never lied, so He always told the truth. But the truth wasn't what those Jews wanted to hear, so they did not believe Him. Sound familiar, like anything in our culture today?

We know from a few chapters later in John that Jesus Himself is the truth. "Jesus answered, 'I am the way and the truth and the life. No one comes to the Father except through me.'" (**John 14:6**). If we know Jesus, then we know the way to the Father, the truth about everything, and we can have life through Him. He is the truth. **1 John 5:20** says, "We know also that the Son of God has come and has given us understanding, so that we may know him who is true.

And we are in him who is true by being in his Son Jesus Christ. He is the true God and eternal life."

A few chapters later, in Jesus' message to His disciples, He shares that the Spirit we have received is the Spirit of truth. "But when he, the Spirit of truth, comes, he will guide you into all the truth. He will not speak on his own; he will speak only what he hears, and he will tell you what is yet to come" (**John 16:13**). The Holy Spirit helps us understand and comprehend what the truth is, because the Spirit is truth.

The belt of truth is part of the armor of God, in **Ephesians 6:14**. We are to have it buckled around our waist. The belt is where a soldier would carry his weapons, so we get our weapons of spiritual warfare from the belt of truth, God's Word.

Speaking truthfully is important for all believers, and it's even part of the Ten Commandments: "You shall not give false testimony against your neighbor" (**Exodus 20:16**). This is echoed many times in the book of Proverbs, too. **Proverbs 12:19** says, "Truthful lips endure forever, but a lying tongue lasts only a moment." **Proverbs 12:22** says, "The Lord detests lying lips, but he delights in people who are trustworthy." **Proverbs 19:5** says, "A false witness will not go unpunished, and whoever pours out lies will not go free." Similarly, **Psalm 15:1-3** says, "Lord, who may dwell in your sacred tent? Who may live on your holy mountain? The one whose walk is blameless, who does what is righteous, who speaks the truth from their heart; whose tongue utters no slander, who does no wrong to a neighbor, and casts no slur on others."

Proverbs 30:5 also tells us that God's Word is true: "Every word of God is flawless; he is a shield to those who take refuge in him." In **John 17:17**, when Jesus is praying to the Father for the disciples, He says, "Sanctify them by the truth; your word is truth." The message of Jesus is truth: "And you also were included in Christ when you heard the message of truth, the gospel of your salvation" (**Ephesians 1:13**).

There are many more passages about truth in the Bible; these are just scratching the surface. Why are there so many? I believe that's partly because the Bible IS truth. The Bible is THE authority, the standard by which we measure whether all things are true or false. Naturally, to hold that place of authority, the Bible must speak about truth. Also, the Bible is the way that God has specifically revealed Himself to us. God is truth, so His Word is truth, and again it should speak on what truth is.

What is truth in your life? Do you try and make your own "truth," or are you holding to the truth of the Bible? I encourage you to find out more about what the Bible says about truth and what the Bible says the truth is.

What the Bible Says About
Love

They say that love makes the world go 'round, and that love is all you need. But what does the Bible say about love?

That's an interesting question to answer, because the Bible is God's Word given to us, revealing who God is. God is love, so the Bible is technically all about God's love. It's like the transient property in math (yes, I'm a geek): if A=B and B=C, then A=C. So if the Bible = God and God = love, then the Bible = love.

Think about it; every story we read in the Bible has to do with God's love. God loved humankind so much that He created us and the world we live in. God loved humankind so much that he at least saved Noah and his family from the Flood so they could repopulate the earth. God loved us so much that He made a covenant with Abraham and made him into a great nation. God loved that great nation, the people of Israel, so much that He kept sending them judges and prophets to turn them back toward following Him when they'd stray. God loved the world so much that He sent Jesus to die and be raised again for us so we could have eternal life (**John 3:16**). God loved us so much that He gave us His Word so we could be equipped to do His work on this earth (**2 Timothy 3:16-17**). The entire Bible shows us God's love!

But the Bible does talk specifically about love in many places as well. The most common place is what's known as the "love chapter" of **1 Corinthians 13**. I encourage you to go read the entire chapter, but I'll highlight a few verses for you here: "Love is patient, love is kind. It does not envy, it does not boast, it is not proud. It does not dishonor others, it is not self-seeking, it is not easily angered, it keeps no record of wrongs. Love does not delight in evil but rejoices with the truth. It always protects, always trusts, always hopes, always perseveres. Love never fails" (**1 Corinthians 13:4-8**).

Another often-quoted passage about love is **1 John 4:7-12**: "Dear friends, let us love one another, for love comes from God. Everyone who loves has been born of God and knows God. Whoever does not love does not know God, because God is love. This is how God showed his love among us: He sent his one and only Son into the world that we might live through him. This is love: not that we loved God, but that he loved us and sent his Son as an atoning sacrifice for our sins. Dear friends, since God so loved us, we also ought to love one another. No one has ever seen God; but if we love one another, God lives in us and his love is made complete in us."

In **John 13:34-35**, Jesus commands us to love one another: "A new command I give you: Love one another. As I have loved you, so you must love one another. By this everyone will know that you are my disciples, if you love one another." Jesus reiterates this command to His disciples in **John 15:12-14**: "My command is this: Love each other as I have loved you. Greater love has no one than this: to lay down one's life for one's friends. You are my friends if you do what I command." While this was a new command in light of the love that Jesus brought to earth, this was also a very old command for the Israelites. **Deuteronomy 6:4-5** (known as the "shema" in Hebrew) says, "Hear, O Israel: The Lord our God, the Lord is one. Love the Lord your God with all your heart and with all your soul and with all your strength."

The Bible also tells about love in human relationships, including that of a husband and wife. **Ephesians 5:25-33** talks about this, as does the book of **Song of Songs**. **Ephesians 4:15-16** highlights how we should interact with others: "Instead, speaking the truth in love, we will grow to become in every respect the mature body of him who is the head, that is, Christ. From him the whole body, joined and held together by every supporting ligament, grows and builds itself up in love, as each part does its work."

Galatians 5:22-23 tells us that love is one of the fruit of the Spirit: "But the fruit of the Spirit is love, joy, peace, forbearance, kindness, goodness, faithfulness, gentleness and self-control. Against such things there is no law." When we have God's Holy Spirit dwelling in us, all of these things will flow from our lives and the Spirit working through us.

There are even Proverbs written about love. For example, **Proverbs 17:9** says, "Whoever would foster love covers over an offense, but whoever repeats the matter separates close friends." **Proverbs 17:17** says, "A friend loves at all times, and a brother is born for a time of adversity."

I could go on and on with more passages about love in the Bible, but as I started with, the whole Bible tells us about God and His love, either directly or indirectly. I'll leave you with one final passage to close this topic.

"For I am convinced that neither death nor life, neither angels nor demons, neither the present nor the future, nor any powers, neither height nor depth, nor anything else in all creation, will be able to separate us from the love of God that is in Christ Jesus our Lord" (**Romans 8:38-39**).

What the Bible Says About
Parenting

This is an interesting piece for me to write since I'm not a parent, at least not of humans anyway - our household does have 5 indoor cats, 4 pet frogs, 2 bearded dragons, and 1 betta fish. This is not a topic I've looked into much considering I don't have a personal need for it in my life, but here's what I've found on what the Bible says about parenting.

The most often-quoted verse I've heard on this topic is **Proverbs 22:6**: "Start children off on the way they should go, and even when they are old they will not turn from it." Proverbs also talks about disciplining children, as in **Proverbs 23:13**: "Do not withhold discipline from a child; if you punish them with the rod, they will not die." **Proverbs 29:17** echoes this sentiment: "Discipline your children, and they will give you peace; they will bring you the delights you desire."

Hebrews 12:5-11 further tells us about discipline for children. **Verses 9-10** say, "Moreover, we have all had human fathers who disciplined us and we respected them for it. How much more should we submit to the Father of spirits and live! They disciplined us for a little while as they thought best; but God disciplines us for our good, in order that we may share in his holiness." God disciplines us as His children, so we have His example to follow as earthly parents disciplining our children.

In **Ephesians 6:1-4**, we see instructions to both children and parents: "Children, obey your parents in the Lord, for this is right. 'Honor your father and mother' — which is the first commandment with a promise — 'so that it may go well with you and that you may enjoy long life on the earth.' Fathers, do not exasperate your children; instead, bring them up in the training and instruction of the Lord."

There are similar instructions in **Colossians 3:20-21**: "Children, obey your parents in everything, for this pleases the Lord. Fathers, do not embitter your children, or they will become discouraged."

But, some of the most important parenting commands in the Bible come from the Old Testament. **Deuteronomy 6:6-9** says, "These commandments that I give you today are to be on your hearts. Impress them on your children. Talk about them when you sit at home and when you walk along the road, when you lie down and when you get up. Tie them as symbols on your hands and bind them on your foreheads. Write them on the doorframes of your houses and on your gates." It's very important for you parents to teach God's Word to your children and to tell your children what God has done in your life, so they can see Him working in their own lives.

Joshua 4:20-24 says, "And Joshua set up at Gilgal the twelve stones they had taken out of the Jordan. He said to the Israelites, 'In the future when your descendants ask their parents, 'What do these stones mean?' tell them, 'Israel crossed the Jordan on dry ground.' For the Lord your God dried up the Jordan before you until you had crossed over. The Lord your God did to the Jordan what he had done to the Red Sea when he dried it up before us until we had crossed over. He did this so that all the peoples of the earth might know that the hand of the Lord is powerful and so that you might always fear the Lord your God.'" This passage shows us the importance of handing down the stories of what God has done to future generations, that they may know God's faithfulness.

God is our Father, so while we humans won't be able to perfectly imitate Him, look to His example given to us in the Bible for how to treat your children with Godly love, to help them grow in their understanding and relationship of their heavenly Father.

What the Bible Says About
Sin and Evil

Wouldn't it be great if there were no sin and no evil in this world? That's the way God created it (**Genesis 1:31**), but He also created humans with free will, and the first humans used that free will to disobey God (**Genesis 3**), thus bringing sin and evil into the world. Because of original sin, the disobedience of those first humans has been passed on to everyone who has been born since then. While we are on this earth, we'll have to deal with sin and evil. So, what else does the Bible say about sin and evil?

Google defines sin as "an immoral act considered to be a transgression against divine law." So, sin is anytime we disobey God, based on the rules He has given us in the Bible. Evil is defined by Google as "profound immorality, wickedness, and depravity, especially when regarded as a supernatural force." Evil is basically the manifestation of sin.

I already discussed how sin came into the world, but what is the consequence of that regarding our relationship with God? **Isaiah 59:2** spells it out: "But your iniquities have separated you from your God; your sins have hidden his face from you, so that he will not hear." God is holy, so He cannot be in the presence of sin, so when we disobey Him and sin, we're separated from God.

We know that everyone falls short and sins against God (**Romans 3:23**). If we say we don't sin, we're liars (**1 John 1:8-10**). There is no one who never sins (**Ecclesiastes 7:20**).

In case you don't know what sin is, the Bible provides some helpful lists, such as the Ten Commandments (**Exodus 20:1-17**). Jesus gives us a list of sins in **Mark 7:20-23**: "He went on: 'What comes out of a person is what defiles them. For it is from within, out of a person's heart, that evil thoughts come — sexual immorality, theft, murder, adultery, greed, malice, deceit, lewdness, envy, slander, arrogance and folly. All these evils come from inside and defile a person.'" Another list of sins is in **Galatians 5:19-21**: "The acts of the flesh are obvious: sexual immorality, impurity and debauchery; idolatry and witchcraft; hatred, discord, jealousy, fits of rage, selfish ambition, dissensions, factions and envy; drunkenness, orgies, and the like. I warn you, as I did before, that those who live like this will not inherit the kingdom of God."

John gives us an explanation of those who are of God versus those who are of the devil in 1 **John 3:6-10**: "No one who lives in him keeps on sinning. No one who continues to sin has either seen him or known him. Dear children, do not let anyone lead you astray. The one who does what is right is righteous, just as he is righteous. The one who does what is sinful is of the devil, because the devil has been sinning from the beginning. The reason the Son of God appeared was to destroy the devil's work. No one who is born of God will continue to sin, because God's seed remains in them; they cannot go on sinning, because they have been born of God. This is how we know who the children of God are and who the children of the devil are: Anyone who does not do what is right is not God's child, nor is anyone who does not love their brother and sister."

This explanation from John may be confusing, however, because even when we are children of God, we do continue to mess up and disobey Him. But when we have been born of God, our desire is to sin no longer; this is in contrast to those who are not born of God, who don't really care if they sin or not. So it's really all about our intentions. **Hebrews 10:26** says, "If we deliberately keep on sinning after we have received the knowledge of the truth, no sacrifice for sins is left." We need to try our best for our sin to not be deliberate or intentional, once we know that we are in fact sinning.

The apostle Paul struggled with this as well in **Romans 7:15-20**: "I do not understand what I do. For what I want to do I do not do, but what I hate I do. And if I do what I do not want to do, I agree that the law is good. As it is, it is no longer I myself who do it, but it is sin living in me. For I know that good itself does not dwell in me, that is, in my sinful nature. For I have the desire to do what is good, but I cannot carry it out. For I do not do the good I want to do, but the evil I do not want to do—this I keep on doing. Now if I do what I do not want to do, it is no longer I who do it, but it is sin living in me that does it." We all go through this same struggle of knowing what is right and not being able to do it.

You may be wondering why a loving God would allow sin and evil to enter His perfect creation. God allows humans to have the choice to love Him or not, rather than just blindly loving Him without having another option. That way, our love for Him is genuine. The theological word for the problem of why a loving God allows evil is "theodicy," and you can search the Worldview Warriors blog for more writings on that topic.

We know that the punishment for sinning is death (**Romans 6:23**), but the second half of that verse is the remedy for sin - that God gives us eternal life through Jesus. **1 Peter 2:24** reminds us of this: "He himself bore our sins' in his body on the cross, so that we might die to sins and live for righteousness; 'by his wounds you have been healed.'"

Paul discusses more about how Jesus' sacrifice saves us from our sins in **Romans 5:12-21**. **Verses 18-19** are the key point in that passage: "Consequently, just as one trespass resulted in condemnation for all people, so also one righteous act resulted in justification and life for all people. For just as through the disobedience of the one man the many were made sinners, so also through the obedience of the one man the many will be made righteous." All sin entered the world through Adam (and Eve), and we all have the opportunity to be saved from that sin through faith in the death and resurrection of Jesus Christ.

Do you have that faith? Please contact us at Worldview Warriors if you'd like to discuss that more, and we'd love to help guide you to that saving faith, so you, too, can have a restored relationship and eternal life with God.

What the Bible Says About
Self-Control

Self-control is one of those things that's a lot easier said than done. We know what we should do (or not do), but we can't always control ourselves (thanks to sin in the world). So, what does the Bible say about self-control or self-discipline?

The first place I think of is the list of the fruit of the Spirit in **Galatians 5:22-23**: "But the fruit of the Spirit is love, joy, peace, forbearance, kindness, goodness, faithfulness, gentleness and self-control. Against such things there is no law." These fruit are not character qualities that we possess of our own power, but they are evident in our lives when the power of the Holy Spirit is living in us.

We know that self-control comes from God living in us. **2 Timothy 1:7** says, "For the Spirit God gave us does not make us timid, but gives us power, love and self-discipline." Paul's letter to Titus shares that self-control is a quality that leaders in the church must have: "Since an overseer manages God's household, he must be blameless—not overbearing, not quick-tempered, not given to drunkenness, not violent, not pursuing dishonest gain. Rather, he must be hospitable, one who loves what is good, who is self-controlled, upright, holy and disciplined" (**Titus 1:7-8**).

James 1:19-21 shows what a self-controlled life looks like: "My dear brothers and sisters, take note of this: Everyone should be quick to listen, slow to speak and slow to become angry, because human anger does not produce the righteousness that God desires. Therefore, get rid of all moral filth and the evil that is so prevalent and humbly accept the word planted in you, which can save you." Paul also writes about this idea of a self-controlled life in **Colossians 1:28-29**: "He [Jesus] is the one we proclaim, admonishing and teaching everyone with all wisdom, so that we may present everyone fully mature in Christ. To this end I strenuously contend with all the energy Christ so powerfully works in me."

Self-control means being able to deny the sinful desires of our flesh in order to follow God's desires for us. In **Luke 9:23** Jesus says, "Whoever wants to be my disciple must deny themselves and take up their cross daily and follow me." **Titus 2:11-12** echoes this: "For the grace of God has appeared that offers salvation to all people. It teaches us to say 'No' to ungodliness and worldly passions, and to live self-controlled, upright and godly lives in this present age." **Romans 8:13** similarly says, "For if you live according to the flesh, you will die; but if by the Spirit you put to death the misdeeds of the body, you will live."

Paul explains self-control from the perspective of an athlete in **1 Corinthians 9:24-27**: "Do you not know that in a race all the runners run, but only one gets the prize? Run in such a way as to get the prize. Everyone who competes in the games goes into strict training. They do it to get a crown that will not last, but we do it to get a crown that will last forever. Therefore I do not run like someone running aimlessly; I do not fight like a boxer beating the air. No, I strike a blow to my body and make it my slave so that after I have preached to others, I myself will not be disqualified for the prize."

The introduction to the book of Proverbs explains how the whole book teaches us to live a life of right living and self-control: "The proverbs of Solomon son of David, king of Israel: for gaining wisdom and instruction; for understanding words of insight; for receiving instruction in prudent behavior, doing what is right and just and fair" (**Proverbs 1:1-3**). **Proverbs 16:32** says, "Better a patient person than a warrior, one with self-control than one who takes a city." **Proverbs 25:28** tells us that self-control is important to protect ourselves: "Like a city whose walls are broken through is a person who lacks self-control."

How are you doing with self-control in your own life? Call on the power of the Holy Spirit living in you to help you make good, self-controlled decisions in your life.

What the Bible Says About
Patience

Patience is one of those things that we all want to have NOW, right? We don't like to be patient in learning patience in our lives. But as followers of Jesus, we should strive to be patient as the Bible tells us to. So, what does it say?

Just as with self-control that I wrote about in the previous section, patience is one of the fruit of the Spirit listed in **Galatians 5:22-23**. That means that when the Spirit is living in us, the Spirit makes patience evident in our lives, rather than us having to simply try our hardest (and fail) at being patient.

1 Thessalonians 5:14 urges us to be patient with everyone: "And we urge you, brothers and sisters, warn those who are idle and disruptive, encourage the disheartened, help the weak, be patient with everyone." **Ephesians 4:2** echoes that: "Be completely humble and gentle; be patient, bearing with one another in love."

The apostle Paul prayed for patience, among other things, for the people at Colossae: "For this reason, since the day we heard about you, we have not stopped praying for you. We continually ask God to fill you with the knowledge of his will through all the wisdom and understanding that the Spirit gives, so that you may live a life worthy of the Lord and please him in every way: bearing fruit in every good work, growing in the knowledge of God, being strengthened with all power according to his glorious might so that you may have great endurance and patience" (**Colossians 1:9-11**). In that same idea, **Romans 12:12** says, "Be joyful in hope, patient in affliction, faithful in prayer."

The wisdom books of the Old Testament talk a lot about patience. For example, **Proverbs 15:18** says, "A hot-tempered person stirs up conflict, but the one who is patient calms a quarrel." **Psalm 37:7** says, "Be still before the Lord and wait patiently for him; do not fret when people succeed in their ways, when they carry out their wicked schemes." **Ecclesiastes 7:8** tells us, "The end of a matter is better than its beginning, and patience is better than pride." **Proverbs 25:15** says, "Through patience a ruler can be persuaded, and a gentle tongue can break a bone."

How do we get patience? James tells us it is through persevering through trials: "Consider it pure joy, my brothers and sisters, whenever you face trials of many kinds, because you know that the testing of your faith produces perseverance. Let perseverance finish its work so that you may be mature and complete, not lacking anything" (**James 1:2-4**). James again encourages believers to be patient toward the end of his letter: "Be patient, then, brothers and sisters, until the Lord's coming. See how the farmer waits for the land to yield its valuable crop, patiently waiting for the autumn and spring rains. You too, be patient and stand firm, because the Lord's coming is near" (**James 5:7-8**).

We can be thankful that God is patient when it comes to saving His creation, as it says in **2 Peter 3:9**: "The Lord is not slow in keeping his promise, as some understand slowness. Instead he is patient with you, not wanting anyone to perish, but everyone to come to repentance." The "love chapter" of **1 Corinthians 13** tells us in **verse 4** that love is patient, and since God is love that reinforces that God is patient.

What are you doing to grow in patience in your life? Or, what is God doing to help you grow in patience? Be encouraged to be patient as God is patient with us.

"May the God who gives endurance and encouragement give you the same attitude of mind toward each other that Christ Jesus had, so that with one mind and one voice you may glorify the God and Father of our Lord Jesus Christ" (**Romans 15:5-6**).

What the Bible Says About
Joy

It is often said that joy is different than happiness; happiness is temporary and based on circumstances often external to us, while joy is more internal and consistent. Today we're looking at joy, so what does the Bible say about it?

As with the last two sections on self-control and patience, joy is another of the fruit of the Spirit found in **Galatians 5:22-23**. We have joy in our lives when the Spirit lives out joy through our obedience to following God.

The book of Psalms is a book of songs, and joy and rejoicing are fun things to sing about, so many verses in it reference joy.

"You make known to me the path of life; you will fill me with joy in your presence, with eternal pleasures at your right hand" (**Psalm 16:11**).

"The Lord has done it this very day; let us rejoice today and be glad"(**Psalm 118:24**).

"For his anger lasts only a moment, but his favor lasts a lifetime; weeping may stay for the night, but rejoicing comes in the morning"(**Psalm 30:5**).

"My lips will shout for joy when I sing praise to you—I, whom you have delivered" (**Psalm 71:23**).

"The Lord is my strength and my shield; my heart trusts in him, and he helps me. My heart leaps for joy, and with my song I praise him" (**Psalm 28:7**).

The prophet Isaiah explained God's invitation to the people of Israel to be in relationship with Him, after their exile was punishment for turning away from Him. **Isaiah 55:12** shows the joyfulness of turning back to God: "You will go out in joy and be led forth in peace; the mountains and hills will burst into song before you, and all the trees of the field will clap their hands."

Zephaniah also prophesied the people of Israel returning back to God. **Zephaniah 3:14** and **17** describe this joyful experience: "Sing, Daughter Zion; shout aloud, Israel! Be glad and rejoice with all your heart, Daughter Jerusalem! … The Lord your God is with you, the Mighty Warrior who saves. He will take great delight in you; in his love he will no longer rebuke you, but will rejoice over you with singing."

Mary, the mother of Jesus, rejoiced after hearing the news that she would bear the savior of the world. Her entire song is in **Luke 1:46-55**, but it starts out with this: "And Mary said: 'My soul glorifies the Lord and my spirit rejoices in God my Savior'" (**Luke 1:46-47**).

In the parable of the lost sheep in **Luke 15:1-7**, Jesus tells how there is much rejoicing when even one sinner repents and turns to Him. **Verse 7** says, "I tell you that in the same way there will be more rejoicing in heaven over one sinner who repents than over ninety-nine righteous persons who do not need to repent."

Jesus encouraged His disciples (and us) to live out joy in their lives, even in the midst of difficulties. Not long before His crucifixion, He told them, "I have told you this so that my joy may be in you and that your joy may be complete" (**John 15:11**). A little later in the same discourse, He said, "So with you: Now is your time of grief, but I will see you again and you will rejoice, and no one will take away your joy" (**John 16:22**).

The apostle Paul wrote his letter to the Philippians while imprisoned for preaching the Gospel, so it's amazing that he focuses on joy throughout this letter. In the last chapter, he sums up his joy in **Philippians 4:4** by writing, "Rejoice in the Lord always. I will say it again: Rejoice!" Similarly, in **1 Thessalonians 5:16**, Paul simply wrote, "Rejoice always."

Paul keeps reminding the Roman church to be joyful as well. **Romans 12:12** says, "Be joyful in hope, patient in affliction, faithful in prayer." Just a few verses later, **Romans 12:15** says, "Rejoice with those who rejoice; mourn with those who mourn." **Romans 14:17** says, "For the kingdom of God is not a matter of eating and drinking, but of righteousness, peace and joy in the Holy Spirit." **Romans 15:13** says, "May the God of hope fill you with all joy and peace as you trust in him, so that you may overflow with hope by the power of the Holy Spirit."

James tells us in **James 1:2-3** that pure joy comes out of our trials: "Consider it pure joy, my brothers and sisters, whenever you face trials of many kinds, because you know that the testing of your faith produces perseverance." **1 Peter 1:6-7** also echoes this thought: "In all this you greatly rejoice, though now for a little while you may have had to suffer grief in all kinds of trials. These have come so that the proven genuineness of your faith — of greater worth than gold, which perishes even though refined by fire — may result in praise, glory and honor when Jesus Christ is revealed."

Finally, we are reminded in **Hebrews 12:1-2** of the joy that Jesus had in order to accomplish His work on the cross: "Therefore, since we are surrounded by such a great cloud of witnesses, let us throw off everything that hinders and the sin that so easily entangles. And let us run with perseverance the race marked out for us, fixing our eyes on Jesus, the pioneer and perfecter of faith. For the joy set before him he endured the cross, scorning its shame, and sat down at the right hand of the throne of God."

How are you doing with joy in your life? Are you focusing more on temporary happiness, or the eternal joy of know Jesus Christ as your Lord and Savior?

What the Bible Says About
Pride

My grandpa used to ask, "Do you want to see my pride and joy?" Then when you said yes, expecting to see a photo of something dear to his heart, he would show you a picture of a bottle of "Pride" brand furniture wax and "Joy" brand dish soap. (He had a great sense of humor!) Since in the previous section I wrote on what the Bible says about joy and this week I'm writing on pride, it made me think of my grandpa's joke.

What is pride? Google defines pride as, "a feeling or deep pleasure or satisfaction derived from one's own achievements, the achievements of those with whom one is closely associated, or from qualities or possessions that are widely admired." There are two kinds of pride: one kind is a sense of accomplishment in a job well done, and the other is being full of ourselves and giving ourselves more glory than we give God.

Galatians 6:4 says, "Each one should test their own actions. Then they can take pride in themselves alone, without comparing themselves to someone else." **2 Corinthians 7:4** says, "I have spoken to you with great frankness; I take great pride in you. I am greatly encouraged; in all our troubles my joy knows no bounds." These verses are examples of the first kind of pride, in which we are pleased with the accomplishments of ourselves or others.

The other kind of pride, the sinful one, is explained in **Proverbs 8:13**: "To fear the Lord is to hate evil; I hate pride and arrogance, evil behavior and perverse speech." **Psalm 10:4** explains this further: "In his pride the wicked man does not seek him; in all his thoughts there is no room for God." **Proverbs 27:2** says, "Let someone else praise you, and not your own mouth; an outsider, and not your own lips." This pride puts ourselves as #1, not God.

We're told about the consequences of pride in **Proverbs 16:18-19**: "Pride goes before destruction, a haughty spirit before a fall. Better to be lowly in spirit along with the oppressed than to share plunder with the proud." **Proverbs 11:2** says, "When pride comes, then comes disgrace, but with humility comes wisdom."

While there are numerous proverbs relating to pride, we also see warnings against it in the New Testament. **Galatians 6:3** says, "If anyone thinks they are something when they are not, they deceive themselves." **1 John 2:16** says, "For everything in the world — the lust of the flesh, the lust of the eyes, and the pride of life — comes not from the Father but from the world." **Philippians 2:3-4** says, "Do nothing out of selfish ambition or vain conceit. Rather, in humility value others above yourselves, not looking to your own interests but each of you to the interests of the others." **Romans 12:16** says, "Live in harmony with one another. Do not be proud, but be willing to associate with people of low position. Do not be conceited."

Jesus even told a parable on pride, which is recorded in **Luke 18:9-14**. It tells of two people praying, one a Pharisee who prayed a very proud prayer, and the other a tax collector who prayed a humble prayer. In **verse 14**, the parable ends with Jesus saying, "For all those who exalt themselves will be humbled, and those who humble themselves will be exalted."

The first century church in Laodicea had their sin of pride addressed by Jesus in the book of Revelation. **Revelation 3:17** says, "You say, 'I am rich; I have acquired wealth and do not need a thing.' But you do not realize that you are wretched, pitiful, poor, blind and naked."

How are you doing with pride in your life? Are you giving God the glory where it is due to Him, or are you taking that glory for yourself?

What the Bible Says About
Music

Music is important in the lives of many people. I have talented musicians in my family, and while I am not one of them, I definitely enjoy good music and attending concerts, musicals, etc. Many people can make a living off their music, and for many others it's a great hobby. Most churches use music in their worship services as another way to praise God. So, it's no surprise that music is addressed in the Bible.

The very first musical reference in the Bible was of Jubal in **Genesis 4:20-21**: "Adah gave birth to Jabal; he was the father of those who live in tents and raise livestock. His brother's name was Jubal; he was the father of all who play stringed instruments and pipes."

The book of Psalms is full of songs, since "psalm" is another word for "song." We no longer have the original tunes for these songs, just the lyrics, but many of today's worship songs use lines from the psalms. The book of Psalms is the longest book in the Bible, actually making up 7% of the total Bible! King David wrote many of the psalms, and in **2 Samuel 23:1** he is called "the hero of Israel's songs."

The book of **Song of Songs** is naturally another musically-oriented book. There are also song lyrics recorded in **Revelation 5:9-10**, **Revelation 7:9-12**, and **Revelation 15:1-4**. Mary the mother of Jesus sang a song of praise in **Luke 1:46-55** after finding out she would bear the Messiah. Moses and his sister Miriam sang a song recorded in **Exodus 15** after God defeated the Egyptian army in the Red Sea. David's victory over Goliath was celebrated with a song in **1 Samuel 18:6-7**.

We see that Jesus and His disciples sang in **Matthew 26:30**, and Paul and Silas sang hymns in prison in **Acts 16:25**. **Ephesians 5:18-20** encourages the church to "speak to one another with psalms, hymns, and songs from the Spirit." **Colossians 3:16** says, "Let the message of Christ dwell among you richly as you teach and admonish one another with all wisdom through psalms, hymns, and songs from the Spirit, singing to God with gratitude in your hearts." **James 5:13** also tells us to sing songs of praise: "Is anyone among you in trouble? Let them pray. Is anyone happy? Let them sing songs of praise."

There are many times that music goes along with other activities told about in the Bible. For example, music was used at the coronation of King Solomon (**1 Kings 1:39-40**), and musicians were in the king's court for his pleasure (**Ecclesiastes 2:8**). Music was used to bring down the walls of Jericho (**Joshua 6**), and David played his harp to calm down King Saul (**1 Samuel 16:14-23**).

Music, like any form of entertainment, can be used for God's glory or against Him. Our motivation and the choices we make regarding music are key to determining which side of this we're on. How are you using music to glorify God in your life?

What the Bible Says About
Leaders

For some inspiration to start writing this post, I searched online for "quotes on leadership" and wow - there are tons! When there's a link titled "620 Leadership Quotes That Will Make You Feel Unstoppable," you know there's a lot of quotable phrases out there on the topic. There are also many, many books on leadership, both from Christian and secular viewpoints, and I even took a class in seminary on Christian Leadership. But, for those of us who consider the Bible to be our primary source of authority, what does it say about leaders?

If we consider ourselves to be followers of Jesus Christ, then He is our ultimate leader. Jesus gives us the best example of servant leadership in **John 13:13-17**, right after He washed the disciples' feet: "You call me 'Teacher' and 'Lord,' and rightly so, for that is what I am. Now that I, your Lord and Teacher, have washed your feet, you also should wash one another's feet. I have set you an example that you should do as I have done for you. Very truly I tell you, no servant is greater than his master, nor is a messenger greater than the one who sent him. Now that you know these things, you will be blessed if you do them." A leader is one who can humble themselves to even the most menial tasks when needed.

This idea of being a humble leader is also explained by Jesus in **Mark 10:42-45**: "You know that those who are regarded as rulers of the Gentiles lord it over them, and their high officials exercise authority over them. Not so with you. Instead, whoever wants to become great among you must be your servant, and whoever wants to be first must be slave of all. For even the Son of Man did not come to be served, but to serve, and to give his life as a ransom for many."

In some of his letters, Paul provides us with character qualities of good leaders. **Titus 1:6-9** says, "An elder must be blameless, faithful to his wife, a man whose children believe and are not open to the charge of being wild and disobedient. Since an overseer manages God's household, he must be blameless — not overbearing, not quick-tempered, not given to drunkenness, not violent, not pursuing dishonest gain. Rather, he must be hospitable, one who loves what is good, who is self-controlled, upright, holy and disciplined. He must hold firmly to the trustworthy message as it has been taught, so that he can encourage others by sound doctrine and refute those who oppose it." **1 Timothy 3:1-13** provides a similar description.

In **Exodus 18**, Moses got a lesson on leadership from his father-in-law Jethro. Moses was trying to handle every dispute that came up among the massive nation of Israel, and it was just too much for him. Jethro urged Moses to appoint additional judges: "But select capable men from all the people — men who fear God, trustworthy men who hate dishonest gain — and appoint them as officials over thousands, hundreds, fifties and tens" (**verse 21**). This is a great example of delegating, with those judges handling the smaller cases and only bringing the more difficult ones up to Moses. We still apply this principle in organizations and governments today.

The Bible is full of stories of leaders, some good and some bad, and there are too many to list all of the stories here. You can find many of these in the book *Heroes of the Faith* written by Logan Ames.

Romans 12:9-13 is about living out our love for others, but it's also a good description of what a leader should do: "Love must be sincere. Hate what is evil; cling to what is good. Be devoted to one another in love. Honor one another above yourselves. Never be lacking in zeal, but keep your spiritual fervor, serving the Lord. Be joyful in hope, patient in affliction, faithful in prayer. Share with the Lord's people who are in need. Practice hospitality."

While we may be leaders among people, the most important thing to remember is that we're all called to be followers (disciples) of Jesus Christ. Even the highest leader here on earth still has to submit to the Almighty Leader, God Himself. Where better to learn our leadership skills from than the One who is truly in charge!

What the Bible Says About
Followers

In the last section, I wrote on what the Bible says about leaders, so to follow that up (pun intended), this week I'm writing on what the Bible says about followers.

Really, the whole Bible is about followers. From the very beginning, humans were created to be in fellowship with God (**Genesis 1:26-27**) and to be obedient to what God calls us to do. That got a lot more difficult after sin entered the world (**Genesis 3**), of course. Humans were also created with free will, which we used to disobey God and not follow His ways. We're all following something, but the question is what or who are we following?

If we claim to be Christians, then we should be following Jesus Christ. This is also known as being His disciples. There are many passages that detail what that looks like, so I'll highlight a few of them here.

"As they were walking along the road, a man said to him, 'I will follow you wherever you go.'
Jesus replied, 'Foxes have dens and birds have nests, but the Son of Man has no place to lay his head.'
He said to another man, 'Follow me.'
But he replied, 'Lord, first let me go and bury my father.'
Jesus said to him, 'Let the dead bury their own dead, but you go and proclaim the kingdom of God.'
Still another said, 'I will follow you, Lord; but first let me go back and say goodbye to my family.'
Jesus replied, 'No one who puts a hand to the plow and looks back is fit for service in the kingdom of God'" (**Luke 9:57-62**)

"Then Jesus came to them and said, "All authority in heaven and on earth has been given to me. Therefore go and make disciples of all nations, baptizing them in the name of the Father and of the Son and of the Holy Spirit, and teaching them to obey everything I have commanded you. And surely I am with you always, to the very end of the age" (**Matthew 28:20**).

"If anyone comes to me [Jesus] and does not hate father and mother, wife and children, brothers and sisters — yes, even their own life — such a person cannot be my disciple. And whoever does not carry their cross and follow me cannot be my disciple" (**Luke 14:26-27**).

"To the Jews who had believed him, Jesus said, 'If you hold to my teaching, you are really my disciples. Then you will know the truth, and the truth will set you free'" (**John 8:31-32**).

"Then Jesus said to his disciples, 'Whoever wants to be my disciple must deny themselves and take up their cross and follow me. For whoever wants to save their life will lose it, but whoever loses their life for me will find it'" (**Matthew 16:24-25**).

From these passages, it's pretty clear that being a follower of Jesus is not necessarily easy. But making the easy choice to follow the world is generally not the best choice in light of eternity, as Jesus taught in **Matthew 7:13-14**: "Enter through the narrow gate. For wide is the gate and broad is the road that leads to destruction, and many enter through it. But small is the gate and narrow the road that leads to life, and only a few find it."

We can learn more about being a follower of Jesus by looking at His first followers and the writings they have left us, including Paul's letters. Paul himself was a great example of a follower of Jesus. As he wrote in **1 Corinthians 11:1**, "Follow my example, as I follow the example of Christ." We should all strive to follow the example of Christ, but we can use other people as examples as well.

But it is important that we are ultimately following only Christ, even as we use others as examples of how to do that. As Paul wrote in **Philippians 3:7-9**, "But whatever were gains to me I now consider loss for the sake of Christ. What is more, I consider everything a loss because of the surpassing worth of knowing Christ Jesus my Lord, for whose sake I have lost all things. I consider them garbage, that I may gain Christ and be found in him, not having a righteousness of my own that comes from the law, but that which is through faith in Christ — the righteousness that comes from God on the basis of faith."

Who or what are you following in this life?

What the Bible Says About
Being Shrewd

The word "shrewd" is kind of a weird word, don't you think? It's not one I use often in my daily speech. But it is a concept taught in the Bible, so today we're going to take a look at what it is.

Google's definition of shrewd is, "having or showing sharp powers of judgment; astute." Some synonyms for shrewd are "astute, sharp-witted, sharp, smart, acute, intelligent, clever, canny, perceptive, perspicacious, sagacious, wise." The idea of being shrewd can be either a positive or a negative thing, depending on the circumstances. You can be shrewd in a crafty way to steal from others, or you can be shrewd in a positive way by making wise choices that help others.

The first Bible passage that comes to my mind when I think of the word shrewd is what's known as the Parable of the Shrewd Manager (sometimes also called the Parable of the Unjust Steward) in **Luke 16:1-13**. In this parable, a wealthy man has a manager or steward to take care of his finances. The manager had been accused of wasting his master's money, so when he's faced with losing his job, the manager calls in each person who owes a debt to his master and decreases those debts, thus making friends with the debtors so they would return the favor to him once he lost his job. The manager then gets commended by his wealthy master for being shrewd since the master sees how the manager used his position to help himself. This is a negative example of being shrewd.

With this parable, Jesus is showing the difference between those who are of the world and those who are believers in Him. We, as followers of Jesus, should use the worldly wealth that we have to build relationships with others and to help them (shrewd in a positive way), not for our own selfish gain like the shrewd manager did (shrewd in a negative way). We should use what we have been given by the master (in our case, God, who has given us all that we have) for the master's purposes, not our own.

Another example of shrewdness is the Parable of the Wise and Foolish Builders found in **Matthew 7:24-27**. The foolish man built his house on sand so it couldn't stand up to the wind and rain, while the wise man built his house on a solid rock foundation and it could withstand whatever came. The wise man was shrewd in a positive way, making intelligent choices that took care of his possessions.

Jesus explains shrewdness also in **Luke 12:42-46**, with a similar account recorded in **Matthew 24:45-51**. Luke 12:42-46 says, "The Lord answered, 'Who then is the faithful and wise manager, whom the master puts in charge of his servants to give them their food allowance at the proper time? It will be good for that servant whom the master finds doing so when he returns. Truly I tell you, he will put him in charge of all his possessions. But suppose the servant says to himself, 'My master is taking a long time in coming,' and he then begins to beat the other servants, both men and women, and to eat and drink and get drunk. The master of that servant will come on a day when he does not expect him and at an hour he is not aware of. He will cut him to pieces and assign him a place with the unbelievers.'" Jesus shows the benefits of being shrewd in a positive way, by taking care of what God has entrusted to us, and the negative consequences of not doing so.

The book of Proverbs also has a number of verses about being shrewd or prudent. **Proverbs 12:23** says, "The prudent keep their knowledge to themselves, but a fool's heart blurts out folly." **Proverbs 13:16** says, "All who are prudent act with knowledge, but fools expose their folly." **Proverbs 18:15** says, "The heart of the discerning acquires knowledge, for the ears of the wise seek it out."

How are you being shrewd in your own life? Are you being positively shrewd or negatively shrewd?

What the Bible Says About
Science

The topic of science and the Bible, and the agreement or disagreement between the two, often comes up in the context of the origins debate of creation versus evolution. I'll leave that discussion to others who are much more experienced and knowledgeable in it, but I will take a look at what the Bible says about science.

First of all, what is science? While there are lots of areas to science, simply put it is observing, studying, experimenting, and learning about the world around us and how it works. Today we have biology, chemistry, physics, etc., but these were all named long after the Bible was written, so there is no direct mention in the Bible of science. But the Bible still talks about the concepts of science.

There are many passages in the Bible where we see the writers observing God's creation. **Psalm 111:2** says, "Great are the works of the Lord; they are pondered by all who delight in them." **Psalm 19:1-6** tells of the wonders God has created in this world for us to observe: "The heavens declare the glory of God; the skies proclaim the work of his hands. Day after day they pour forth speech; night after night they reveal knowledge. They have no speech, they use no words; no sound is heard from them. Yet their voice goes out into all the earth, their words to the ends of the world. In the heavens God has pitched a tent for the sun. It is like a bridegroom coming out of his chamber, like a champion rejoicing to run his course. It rises at one end of the heavens and makes its circuit to the other; nothing is deprived of its warmth."

The Bible also has passages that refer to scientific concepts that we have since proven to be true. For example, **Isaiah 40:22** indicates that the earth is round, **Job 26:7** tells how the earth seems to float in space, **Ecclesiastes 1:6** tells about wind currents, and **Psalm 8:8** and **Isaiah 43:16** indicate that there are currents in the sea.

The Bible has a lot to say about knowledge, and science is really just the search for more knowledge regarding how our world works. We know that God has all knowledge, and as we seek out God we will be seeking more knowledge of Him and of how our world works. **Proverbs 25:2** says, "It is the glory of God to conceal a matter; to search out a matter is the glory of kings." **Colossians 2:2-3** says, "My goal is that they may be encouraged in heart and united in love, so that they may have the full riches of complete understanding, in order that they may know the mystery of God, namely, Christ, in whom are hidden all the treasures of wisdom and knowledge." **Job 38-40** tells about all the mysteries of God's creation that mankind will likely never know.

King Solomon ponders the idea of science and knowledge in **Ecclesiastes 1:13-17**: "I applied my mind to study and to explore by wisdom all that is done under the heavens. What a heavy burden God has laid on mankind! I have seen all the things that are done under the sun; all of them are meaningless, a chasing after the wind. What is crooked cannot be straightened; what is lacking cannot be counted. I said to myself, 'Look, I have increased in wisdom more than anyone who has ruled over Jerusalem before me; I have experienced much of wisdom and knowledge.' Then I applied myself to the understanding of wisdom, and also of madness and folly, but I learned that this, too, is a chasing after the wind."

The Bible is not a science textbook; it is a book that tells us all about the God who created science and everything that we can observe and even many things we can't yet observe. We humans are curious by nature, so we'll continue seeking out answers to the mysteries of this world. But more importantly, seek out a relationship with the Creator who made it!

What the Bible Says About
Angels

One topic many people wonder about is angels. Do they exist? What are they like? Are they good or evil? Do we have guardian angels? While we may not have all the answers to those questions, here we'll take a look at what the Bible says about angels.

We know that there are both good angels and evil angels, known as demons. Based on how many times angels or demons are referenced in the Bible, we can say with certainty that they do exist.

We know that angels and demons both possess intelligence, as seen in **Matthew 8:29** and **1 Peter 1:12**. They show emotion, as we read in **Luke 2:13** and **James 2:19**. They also have a will that they can use, as in **Luke 8:28-31**, **2 Timothy 2:26**, and **Jude 1:6**.

Hebrews 1:14 tells us, "Are not all angels ministering spirits sent to serve those who will inherit salvation?" Angels are spirit beings without physical bodies. They still have identities even without bodies. God sends angels to help human believers.

Since angels are created beings, they do not have the unlimited knowledge of God. In reference to the coming judgment day, **Matthew 24:36** tells us, "But about that day or hour no one knows, not even the angels in heaven, nor the Son, but only the Father."

What do angels do with their time? One of their primary activities is praising and worshiping God. **Psalm 148:2** says, "Praise him, all his angels; praise him, all his heavenly hosts." **Hebrews 1:6** says, "And again, when God brings his firstborn into the world, he says, 'Let all God's angels worship him.'" **Revelation 5:8-13** also shows us a scene of angels worshipping God in heaven.

Along with praising God, angels also serve God. **Psalm 103:20** tells us, "Praise the Lord, you his angels, you mighty ones who do his bidding, who obey his word." They help carry out God's judgments, as we see in **Revelation 7:1** and **8:2**. In **Acts 12:5-10**, it is an angel who appears to Peter and releases him from prison.

Angels also deliver God's messages. In fact, the word used for angel in Greek is the same word as messenger. In **Luke 1:11**, an angel appears to Zechariah and tells him he's going to be a father to John the Baptist. Later in that chapter, **Luke 1:26-38** records the angel Gabriel telling Mary she would be the mother of the Messiah.

We do not know how many angels there are. The Bible mentions a "host" of angels, such as when they appeared to the shepherds to tell them of Jesus' birth in **Luke 2:8-15**. The ones specifically named in the Bible are Gabriel and Michael. Gabriel delivered messages to Daniel regarding the end times in **Daniel 8:15-27** and **9:20-27**. He also delivered news of upcoming babies to Zechariah and Mary as previously mentioned. It is suspected that the angel who visited Joseph in a dream (**Matthew 1:18-25**) was also Gabriel.

The other angel mentioned by name in the Bible is Michael. While Gabriel appears to be more of a messenger angel, Michael is more of a warrior angel. **Jude 1:9** refers to Michael by name as archangel, which means he's the chief angel. When we see Michael mentioned by name in the Bible, it's in a battle scene. This happens in **Daniel 10:21** and **12:1**, as well as **Revelation 12:7-9**. We see Michael's high rank in the angel army because he's leading the troops.

We could also include fallen angels in this list as well. There are two of them – Lucifer/Satan and Apollyon/Abaddon. We see specific references to Lucifer falling from heaven in **Isaiah 14:12-18** and **Luke 10:18**. This is our enemy who seeks to destroy us and draw us away from God (**1 Peter 5:8**). **Revelation 9:11** tells us of Apollyon: "They had as king over them the angel of the Abyss, whose name in Hebrew is Abaddon and in Greek is Apollyon (that is, Destroyer)."

You may have noticed that all of the specific angel names mentioned are masculine. Does that mean all angels are men? Not necessarily. There are no specific passages in the Bible that tell us angels are always male or female, which really means that their gender is not a concern. God Himself is referred to with masculine pronouns, but gender is a human characteristic that He is beyond. The same is likely true for angels, as they are lower than God but higher than humans in the created order (**Hebrews 2:7-9, Psalm 8:4-5**).

What about guardian angels? Do we each have one? That is not clear from Scripture, though we do see that angels are sent to protect us (**Daniel 6:20-23, 2 Kings 6:13-17**) and guide us (**Matthew 1:20-21, Acts 8:26**). The Bible passage often used to give support to guardian angels is **Matthew 18:10**: "See that you do not despise one of these little ones. For I tell you that their angels in heaven always see the face of my Father in heaven." This doesn't clearly tell us that we each have a guardian angel or not, but it seems to imply that God is watching over all of us and sometimes uses the angels to minister to us.

There are many more passages that reference angels and show us the work that angels do. While we may be curious about more specifics, be content to know that angels do exist and are used by God to deliver His messages and carry out His plans when He needs them.

What Does the Bible
Say?

As you've seen throughout this book, the Bible has a lot to say specifically addressing some topics. These would include money, love, miracles, truth, and others. For other topics, the Bible is almost silent, including dinosaurs, aliens from other planets, or entertainment just to name a few. Even for the ones that the Bible does not address directly, we can still use the truths contained in Scripture to guide us on how to follow its teaching on any particular issue.

Personally, I have enjoyed writing on all of these topics, as it gave me good reason to dig deeply into what the Scriptures say about each one of them. I have had the opportunity to be well-educated on the Bible for basically my entire life, but knowing that the Bible speaks on a topic is different than looking into exactly where and how much it addresses that topic. I have been challenged at times with the topics that aren't found as easily in the Scriptures, as well as being challenged on other topics with which of the myriad of passages to include.

As God often does things, some of the topics have been very timely in my life as I have written about them. Sometimes God works in our lives so that a particular topic comes up right when I'm experiencing life that goes along with it. For example, I heard a friend's wife passed away from a long battle with cancer, and that very day I was writing on what the Bible says about life and death.

So, to wrap up this book, I'd like to bring up again what the Bible says about its own authority and why it is so valuable to speak into our lives in every season or issue that comes up.

2 Timothy 3:16-17 says, "All Scripture is God-breathed and is useful for teaching, rebuking, correcting and training in righteousness, so that the servant of God may be thoroughly equipped for every good work."

This passage reminds us that the Bible will "thoroughly equip" us for "every good work." We're not partially equipped for some things, but **fully** equipped for whatever life may throw at us. If you don't feel fully equipped, I challenge you to keep studying! Keep reading the Word for yourself, and supplement that with good, Biblical teaching and study groups. We're always publishing new blog posts at the Worldview Warriors blog, and feel free to connect with us if you have questions on any Bible topics, or even what the Bible says on a topic that I didn't address.

I do hope you have enjoyed this book and have learned new things about how the Bible addresses certain topics. Be encouraged to keep digging deeper into God's Word; it really is the answer for everything.

Equipping Students to Impact This Generation
For Jesus Christ

www.WorldviewWarriors.org

Worldview Warriors
P.O. Box 681
Findlay, OH 45839

info@worldviewwarriors.org
(419) 835-2777

We provide free weekly resources available to use in
personal study, small groups, Sunday school classes, sermons, etc.

Contact us to book Katie Erickson or one of our other speakers
for interviews or your next event!

Find us on Facebook
www.Facebook.com/WorldviewWarriors

DONOTKEEPSILENT

Speaking out the name of Jesus Christ in action and in word

DO NOT KEEP SILENT

We are a talk radio show that plays great music as well for those wanting to grow in their relationship with Christ

90.1 FM - WXML in Upper Sandusky, OH area
Sunday evenings from 7pm - 9pm

Radio4Him online
Wednesday evenings from 7pm - 9pm

We have a 2-hour program and a 30-minute program available

DoNotKeepSilent.com

Facebook.com/DoNotKeepSilent

Made in the USA
Middletown, DE
09 February 2019